THE MOST HOLY TRINOSOPHIA

A BOOK OF THE DEAD

Translation & Introduction by M.R. Osborne

Foreward by Piers A. Vaughan

Library of Congress Control Number: 2021917880

ISBN 978-1-947907-16-4

Rose Circle Publications
P.O. Box 854
Bayonne, NJ 07002, U.S.A.
www.rosecirclebooks.com

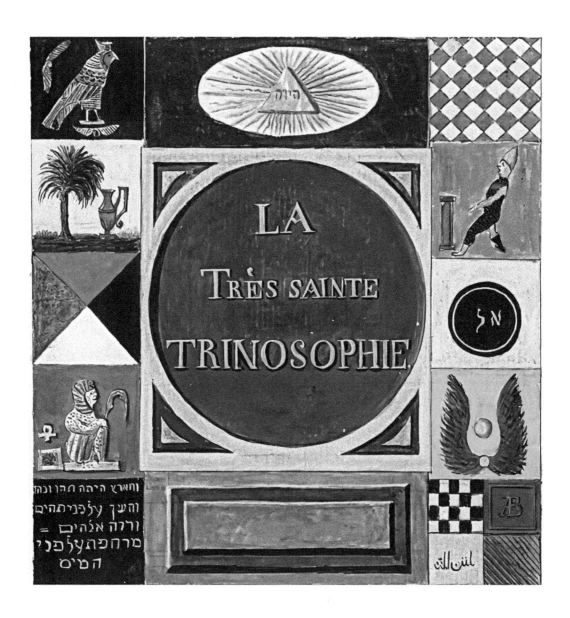

The frontispiece
Photo Médiathèque Jacques-Chirac, Troyes Champagne Métropole

Front cover: Detail of a scribe from the frontispiece
Photo Médiathèque Jacques-Chirac, Troyes Champagne Métropole

CONTENTS

FOREWORD

La Très Sainte Trinosophie, The Most Holy Trinosophia, was described by Manly Palmer Hall as "the rarest of occult manuscripts". It is 88 years since his translation and commentary appeared. A new look at this extraordinary document is overdue. Given the reverence in which Hall is held, why would anyone attempt to do this? I would offer three important reasons.

Firstly, the scholarship of the time tended to be more credulous – or hopeful – than our cynical times. Indeed, Hall appears to have accepted the suggested authorship of Saint-Germain as given (others have attributed the work to Giuseppe Balsamo, Count Cagliostro), without any evidence. We need to revisit this assumption.

Secondly, the resources available to people nearly a century ago were clearly far less complete than those available to us in this age of the internet, international cataloguing and an assembling of precious manuscripts and new discoveries which daily add to the 'Akashic Records' of the World Wide Web. We are seeing a number of respected authors revisiting rituals and previously held beliefs and reinterpreting in the light of what we now know.

Thirdly, we have the aesthetic reason. When Hall first made the texts available to the English-speaking world, the best available images of the extraordinary manuscript in the library at Troyes, France, known as MS2400, were of poor quality, low resolution and black and white. Thanks to the **Institut de Recherche et d'Histoire des Textes** (IRHT), founded in 1937 in France as a part of the **Centre Nationale de la Recherche Scientifique** (CNRS), a massive task was undertaken to study and – more importantly – to make high quality copies of books, parchments documents, papers and papyrus manuscripts from antiquity to the Renaissance and beyond, including all such finds in the Mediterranean basin. Over the years, and using increasingly sophisticated equipment, they have made available images of earlier documents of extraordinary clarity and fidelity, which are extensively used in the academic field for study. These are now made available in this book with the express permission of the IRHT and the Bibliothèque de Troyes.

The attribution of the manuscript to Saint Germain is due to a bookseller's note pasted to the front of the manuscript, which, without further proof, remains moot. Indeed, as a personal example, when I obtained an first edition copy of Louis-Claude de Saint-Martin's "*Des Erreurs et de la Verité*" from a bookstore in the South of France, it was listed under 'Medical' texts, no doubt because the bookseller, not realizing the importance of the book, had opened it at random and come across a comment about 18th Century medicine!

The translator has taken great pains to offer a book which, rather than being a dry academic resumé of the origins of the book, is an opportunity to experience the book as those would have done for the first time when it came to light. As well as providing an enlightening Introduction, in which he compares the book to the Egyptian Book of the Dead, and discusses a number of theories concerning the book, given the further knowledge we have acquired in the intervening years from the 1930s, he presents the book in its entirety as a medium for contemplation and meditation. I particularly like the fact that he has given the work such prominence in the book, placing it immediately after his initial commentary, instead of relegating it to an Appendix. This allows the reader to gain some signposts from his expert commentary, before moving directly into gaining personal insight from the images in the book.

Indeed, the book should be *experienced*, then studied in its original form before moving onto the translation, which now has an opportunity to be used as a supportive tool, rather than as the immediate purpose of this translation. This way the reader will have an opportunity to contemplate what the images mean to him or her, before reading the accompanying text. In a way this translation benefits the anglophone over the francophone, since it allows this intermediate step to take place without the intervention of words.

There is little point going over the contents of the book in detail, since that would be no more than repetition. Perhaps the most salient point to raise is the fact of how dated Hall's book seems in light of our present ability, not to critique his work, but to finally see the manuscript as it originally looked, and to understand how using the poor black and white pages to which he had access gave rise to problems both in translation and interpretation. Rather than labour these points, the author has contented himself with pointing out the error made by the original translator in reading the name of the recipient of these important instructions, and how a single letter can change the meaning of that name. Another issue is that of interpreting words which were written in Hebrew, in Greek, in Sanskrit, in Arabic and in codes. Indeed, I suggest to the author that he leave these translations in the hands of Hall, knowing that it would be an impossible task to decipher the clear errors in these words. The teachings are no less profound for this, even if one of two word-games have been missed.

It has been over eighty years since Manly Palmer Hall presented this work to the English-speaking world. Now, with the amazing advances in technology and the skills of M. R. Osborne, we have a chance to experience this book in its original glory and rediscover its alchemical secrets for ourselves.

Piers A. Vaughan
September 2021

INTRODUCTION

La Très Sainte Trinosophie, The Most Holy Trinosophia, or The Most Holy Threefold Wisdom is an occult work of the late eighteenth-century. Described by the National Library of France as "very carefully executed", the book measures some nine and a half by twelve inches in a quarto format. It is bound in red Moroccan leather, and contains ninety-nine paper leaves divided into twelve sections, each with a beautiful watercolour illustration. The initial letters of each paragraph are also hand painted, and there are twenty-four illustrated vignettes and triangular graphical pendants marking the end of each section.

The manuscript incorporates an eclectic mix of esoteric symbolism and ciphers, drawn from several of the occult schools including alchemy and Hebraic kabbala. The illustrations contain text composed in a variety of ancient languages, and much of the symbolism incorporates concepts independent of any known linguistic expression. In short, the Trinosophia is an anomaly, and one of the most profound and challenging of all esoteric manuscripts.[1]

There are diverse theories regarding what constitutes the key theme of the work, ranging from an allegorical masonic initiation to a prophesy or auger relating to

---

[1] "In all my twenty years of experience as a reader of archaic writings, I have never encountered such ingenious codes and methods of concealment as are found in this manuscript. In only a few instances are complete phrases written in the same alphabet; usually two or three forms of writing are employed, with letters written upside down, reversed, or with the text written backwards. Vowels are often omitted, and at times several letters are missing with merely dots to indicate their number." – Manly P. Hall, *The Most Holy Trinosophia of the Comte de St.-Germain with Introductory Material and Commentary*, Los Angeles, The Phoenix Press, 1933 p.31.

the end of the world. These theories are as little established as the debate over the book's authorship. Indeed, nothing of any particular merit has been published concerning the manuscript since Manly P. Hall's seminal self-published commentary of 1933.[2] Hall's work remains the leading authority to this day but, as with most English language editions, only reproduced the illustrations in black and white, thereby losing the vibrancy of this incredibly rare and beautiful manuscript. Largely overlooked in Hall's commentary is the Trinosophia's relationship with The Egyptian Book of the Dead. While this present edition intentionally avoids an exegesis of the entire manuscript, some consideration of its connection with Egyptian religion is required if one is to understand the book at all.

The fifth and sixth sections of the manuscript provide an explanation of the principal purpose of the work. It is contended that the Trinosophia is an abridged version of the ancient Egyptian Book of the Dead, a provenance derived from the Graeco-Egyptian Hermeticism from which Western alchemy arose. Notwithstanding this, a commentary on each section of the manuscript is not provided for another reason: namely to encourage the reader to meditate on the illustrations, and to find his or her own meaning in them. This is an important esoteric exercise, since The Most Holy Trinosophia is above all a mystical work, and therein lies the correct approach to it.

---

[2] *ibid.*

The text and the colour illustrations provided in this edition are high resolution images of the original manuscript, held at the Médiatheque Jacques Chirac Metropolitan Library at Troyes, France. They are reproduced here with the Library's express permission.

The Imagination

The Quest or *magnum opus*[3] of the modern era is essentially one of self-initiation. It is an intensely personal journey, much like birth and death, since the individuation of people today is such that collective and/or third-party initiation is, in truth, no longer required. Given sufficient time the self-initiate will find the Most Holy Trinosophia an invaluable resource. The reason for this is that the book provides a key to unlock our conscious imagination, one of the three intellectual wisdoms unique to man.[4] The initiate's path thus begins with the development of a fundamental mood of reverence upon reading the book, which in turn produces a desire for self-improvement and ever greater knowledge.

The Most Holy Trinosophia is perhaps the most inspiring of all the alchemical manuscripts, because this beautiful book speaks to the soul through the imagination. The illustrations help develop definite inner qualities of perception, in a way that few other esoteric materials achieve. Therein lies the secret of the manuscript's survival in the final years of the Counter Reformation, and its relevance in modern times. In psychological terms, the conscious mind will, over

---

[3] *The Great Work*: the path of the initiate.
[4] Reason and memory being the others.

time, discover a deeper meaning in the contemplation of sacred imagery because such impressions influence our subconscious. This observation reminds us of the Jungian doctrine of Archetypal Ideas, wherein images and symbols correspond with the primal or unconscious imagination. If allowed time and space to develop, this juxtaposition between the conscious and unconscious imagination will inevitably open higher tiers of clairvoyance. As Jung stated:

"In the darkness of anything external to me I find, without recognizing it as such, an interior or psychic life that is my own ... I am therefore inclined to assume that the real route of alchemy is sought less in philosophical doctrines than in the projections of individual investigators."[5] Carl Jung

Influenced by Jung, the Czech psychologist Stanislav Grof differentiated between everyday modes of consciousness – such as those which concerned commonplace reality – and that which he termed the "mystical state". Grof's experimental psychology induced non-ordinary levels of consciousness in his patients, such that they perceived different experiences of reality. In the early stages of his research these higher states were accomplished using the platform of psychedelics, but Grof later came to focus on meditation techniques. His conclusion was that the mystical or "holotropic" state corresponded with the Divine or "Brahman" consciousness, which lies behind the teaching of all mystical schools. Grof would write:

---

[5] *Psychology and Alchemy*, Jung, C.G., London 1953 p.245.

"The fact that so many different cultures throughout human history have found shamanic techniques useful and relevant suggests that the holotropic states engage what the anthropologists call the "primal mind," a basic and primordial aspect of the human psyche that transcends race, gender, culture, and historical period."[6] Stanislav Grof

The barrier between everyday reality and what we term clairvoyance (the ability to perceive objective realities beyond our physical senses), begins to break down in the appreciation of art and nature. For instance, we may recall a time when a picture or a similar, external object gave rise to a sense of reverence within us, leading to an awareness of the numinous. Occasionally we may find ourselves going back again to that source of inspiration. For me such contact with the numinous in art first occurred when I encountered, quite by chance, the three life-size Chinese Luohan sculptures at the British Museum.[7] Long before I understood that these figures signify the aspiration for enlightenment, I visited them at every available opportunity, often returning late to work. Indeed, I subsequently discovered these sculptures have a reputation for engendering similar effects in other people. How is it that certain art, particularly of a devotional kind, has such an impact on the mind? The answer may lie in our shared experience of the numinous, which is something very core indeed. It comes as no surprise that art awakens a long-forgotten spiritual memory within us, because it also represents the stylised memory of the artist; with whose own

---

[6] *The Way of the Psychonaut Volume One: Encyclopedia for Inner Journeys*, Grof, S., 2019.
[7] These clay sculptures date from AD 907 – 1125.

mind we make a direct connection. Jung experienced this sense of mystery, but never came close to fully understanding it:

> *"The years ... when I pursued the inner images were the most important of my life. Everything else is to be derived from this. It began at that time, and the later details hardly matter anymore. My entire life consisted in elaborating what had burst forth from the unconscious and flooded me like an enigmatic stream and threatened to break me. That was the stuff and material for more than only one life."*[8] Carl Jung

The Most Holy Trinosophia was written by an esoteric master of incomparable insight and understanding. It is therefore not long in contemplation of it before feelings of reverence can arise within us. Clairvoyants, so we are told, often try to convey what they 'see' of the spiritual world through their feelings, in place of the physical organs of perception. It is as if merely by smelling a rose they can 'see' the colour without sight of it. If spiritual realms beyond our ordinary senses do indeed exist, then perhaps they are experienced by awakening a primeval third sight long since lost in waking, ordinary existence. With the right approach to it, the Most Holy Trinosophia can operate as a working tool to reacquire these latent abilities. On one level this is its true significance; another is that it acts as a guide for what lies ahead, beyond the grave.

---

[8] Carl Jung in conversation with Aniela Joffe about the Red Book or Liber Novus, in 1957.

Authorship

Speculative theories concerning the Trinosophia's authorship have long arisen and are a fascinating area of conjecture and ongoing debate. We may never know if one or more people were involved in its composition. Nonetheless, most of the versions available in print today attribute the book to the mysterious Comte de Saint-Germain (1691 or 1712-1784), whose ownership was 'proved' by the discovery of a sales slip accompanying the only known surviving copy (the manuscript held at the Municipal Library in Troyes, which attributes the text to him in its catalogue).

The untitled and contemporaneous grimoire known as the 'Triangular Book of Saint-Germain'[9] is similarly attributed to this enigmatic raconteur of the French royal court. The Triangular Book is written entirely in cipher and was originally accompanied by another manuscript containing the key to them. It is possible that The Most Holy Trinosophia may also have had an accompanying volume, although there is no evidence of this. Neither is there any convincing proof the manuscript was written by Saint-Germain, other than the note at the head of the manuscript under the *nom de plume* of one Philotaume,[10] stating that his copy is "the only existing work of the Count de Saint-Germain."

---

[9] *Ex Dono Sapientissimi Comitis St. Germain Qui Orbem Terrarum Per Curcurrit.*
[10] Like Philocale, this is a mystical name. Indeed, *Philocales* means a lover of good, while *Philotimos* means a lover of honour.

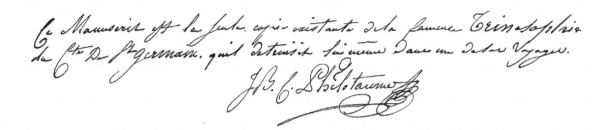

Photo Médiathèque Jacques-Chirac, Troyes Champagne Métropole

Below this are added the words: "this unique manuscript is the one owned by the Comte di Cagliostro, and which was found in Rome by Massena at the Grand Inquisitor's house." If we reject Saint-Germain's authorship on account of the handwritten citation by the eponymous Philotaume, or wishful thinking on the part of those attached to the idea, then Alessandro Comte di Cagliostro (1743-1795) stands apart as the most likely writer. Both men were known to have met at Holstein and in Paris, and each practised an Egyptianized form of freemasonry popular at the time.

The Triangular Book of the Comte de Saint-Germain

18

It is more likely the manuscript was composed for use in Cagliostro's Egyptian rite, and indeed the only known copy was reputedly confiscated from him upon his arrest in 1789. In the catalogue at the Bibliothèque Nationale de France, Cagliostro is cited as both the manuscript "owner" and as the Sicilian Giuseppe Balsamo, "*aventurier italien et médecin*" (the "Italian adventurer and doctor"). The designation "adventurer" is a vestige of one of the most brutal and systematic character demolition jobs in history. If we may put aside, for a moment, the prejudices of the eighteenth-century Church and the purported origin of Cagliostro as a low-born impostor, fake and fraudster, then his own claim to have spent part of his childhood in Egypt may, perhaps, be vindicated by the content of the Trinosophia itself. There is also simply too much of Alessandro's biographical detail in the opening section of the text to entirely discount his authorship. If we are willing to accept the word of the lawyer who purportedly uncovered evidence of Cagliostro's identity under pressure from the Roman Inquisition, then there is equally no reason to doubt the Comte's own version of his provenance. Why not? In the absence of convincing evidence to the contrary one can make up one's own mind. If we accept Cagliostro's colourful account, then we are left with a man whose knowledge and understanding of the occult was second to none and, more crucially, his understanding of Egyptian hieroglyphs. This is relevant, for, as we shall consider, The Most Holy

Trinosophia bears strong resemblance to the Egyptian Book of the Dead, or the Book Of Coming Forth By Day.[11]

At first sight The Most Holy Trinosophia appears to be an allegorical initiation, with many alchemical symbols embedded within its text and illustrations, leading from the first to sixth and final stage of perfection. The colours of the illustrations are directly connected with the alchemical path of initiation, and the stages of transformation which each step symbolises. If one considers the illustrations in detail, it is also apparent that they constitute much more than a handbook for use in a proto-masonic Egyptian Rite, as there can be few more powerful and emotive themes than those conveyed by the soul's journey from the Gate of Humility to its ascension to the Gate of Heaven. This is the real subject of the work. It is a mysticism which reaches deep into humanity's spiritual memory.

---

[11] *Rau nu Pert em Heru*: lit. "the spell for coming into the spiritual life with Horus."

The Comte de Saint-Germain

Whilst we may never discover the identity of the author, we do know Cagliostro valued and owned The Most Holy Trinosophia. We also know that his Egyptian Rite in freemasonry both challenged and frustrated its opponents to a not inconsiderable degree, thereby earning their enmity. While not evidence of authorship, the preface of the manuscript suggests Cagliostro's influence. Following Cagliostro's imprisonment by the Roman Inquisition in the Castel Sant Angelo[12] and later at the remote Papal prison of Forte San Leo[13], the book was considered lost until its rediscovery towards the end of the Napoleonic Wars.

---

[12] Hadrian's mausoleum, Rome.
[13] One can only marvel at the irony of the name of his last prison and final resting place, given the astrological significance of the key illustration to the manuscript, as we shall see.

Alessandro Comte di Cagliostro
Photo Médiathèque Jacques-Chirac, Troyes Champagne Métropole

The Book of the Dead

The ability to read and decipher Egyptian hieroglyphs was lost around the fifth century AD.[14] The question naturally arises as to how the illustrations and structure of The Most Holy Trinosophia bear such close resemblance to The Egyptian Book of the Dead. The enigma surrounding this cross correspondence only grows deeper when one considers that a complete and de-coded translation of The Book of the Dead did not appear until after Jean-François Champollion's

---

[14] Monumental use of hieroglyphs ceased after the closing of all non-Christian temples in AD 391.

deciphering of the Rosetta Stone in 1830, by the German linguist and Egyptologist Karl Richard Lepsius.[15] Lepsius took on the mantle of completing Champollion's deciphering of hieroglyphics following the latter's death in 1832, and travelled extensively throughout Egypt and the Sudan in order to do so. By 1842 he had translated what we know today as the Book of the Dead, and first coined the phrase *Totenbuch*.[16] This was nearly half a century after Cagliostro's death. While there had been serious attempts at decipherment from the seventeenth century onwards, there was nothing at the time of the appearance of the Trinosophia remotely approaching a complete translation. We know, however, that Cagliostro had been working on his Egyptian Rite in the years leading up to his capture and confiscation of the manuscript.

The Rosetta Stone

[15] 1810-1884.
[16] Lit. the Book of the Dead."

Karl Richard Lepsius (1810-1884)

The Egyptian Book of the Dead is comprised of a collection of over one thousand hieroglyphic characters, developed from an earlier system of pictographs (known as the Pyramid Texts) written between approximately between 1550 and 50 BC. The Book of the Dead is formed into four main parts, each containing chapters containing magical symbols and acoustic invocations. The principal themes are:

* the resurrection body;

* journeyings through the underworld ("Duat");

* a final judgement in the halls of Ausar; and, if successful

- eternal life in the Field of Reeds[17]

Originally a text for Egypt's elite, The Book of the Dead steadily became available to all, regardless of social status. The magical spells and incantations in the hieroglyphs were intended to guide the soul (the *ka*[18] or vital essence) through the various worlds populated by the gods and spirits in Duat. In comparison, The Most Holy Trinosophia is divided into twelve sections or chapters, each representing a sign of the zodiac. The subject matter is also the quest of the soul after physical death for eternal life.

The ancient Egyptian initiate was required to memorise the hieroglyphs and was tasked with living by their moral precepts. His life was therefore spent in constant readiness for death. In so doing, he aimed to attain perfection and immortality in the next life, but which was only possible by developing the inner qualities required to a sufficiently high degree. Eternal life depended on the *intention* of the deceased. Parallels can be drawn with the narrator of The Most Holy Trinosophia bemoaning the great stumbling block of pride, the cause of man's Fall from grace in the Christian tradition:

---

[17] The reed was the symbol of upper Egypt and itself a correspondence between the earthly and heavenly kingdoms. The reed is also the symbol of wisdom and learning, as it was used by the Egyptians for writing. The goddess Seshat, an avatar of the god Thoth, is often shown holding a reed and which may also be likened to a wand.

[18] *Khet* the physical form, *Sah* the spiritual form, *Ib* the heart or mind, *Ka* the vital essence, *Ba* the human personality, *Shut* its shadow, *Shekhem* its form, *Ren* its name, and *Akh* the intellect.

"One moment destroyed everything. I spoke, and everything vanished like a cloud. Oh, my son, do not follow in my footsteps. Do not let any vain desire that shines in the eye of the world cause your downfall."

The description of the underworld in the Trinosophia corresponds closely with the dark Land of the Dead, "shrouded in mist and cloud".[19] Duat is a place of judgment, where the soul takes on the shape or form of its earthly body to embark upon its journey.[20] Central to the cosmogony of both The Most Holy Trinosophia and The Book of the Dead is the belief that the spirit realms follow set laws, just as our natural world does. As Emanuel Swedenborg once said: "things that are in heaven are more real than things that are in the world of man".

The essential point is that the immutable law of God is for each soul to face a final reckoning, however understood. These themes are emphasised in both texts. In The Book of the Dead Osiris (the god of resurrection) and Ra (the god of divination) determine the fate of the soul. Ra acts as the deceased's invisible guide, and it is probably Ra lifting the narrator by the hair in the Trinosophia, for Ra "is all in all", states the Book of the Dead: "from him came, and to him return, the souls of men". There is also a numinous sense in the Trinosophia of a hidden watcher or presence observing the narrator's trials.

---

[19] The Odyssey, Book 11 v.17.
[20] The narrator's experience may be likened to the trial of the Greek hero Odysseus to experience a reality lying beyond his ordinary sense of comprehension.

Hymn to Ra

"I see Horus in the form of the guardian of the rudder. Thoth and Ma'at are upon his two arms. Received am I in the prow of the Mandet Boat[21] and in the stern of the Mseseket Boat[22]. Ra gives divine sight, to see the Aten, to view the moon god unceasingly every day, and the ability of souls to come forth, to walk every place they may desire. Proclaim my name! Find him in the wood board of offerings. There have been given to me offerings in the life-giving presence, as it is given to the followers of Horus. It is done for me in the divine place in the boat on the day of the sailing, the journey of God. I am received in the presence of Osiris in the land of truth speaking of the Ka of Osiris." Hymn to Ra, The Egyptian Book of the Dead

A similar theme of journeying celestial waters and of personal transformation occur in the Trinosophia. In order to progress, the soul must correctly pronounce

---

[21] Ra's evening boat.
[22] Ra's morning boat.

the magical names hidden in the secret ciphers and operate the rituals perfectly. There is little difference in the cosmogony of the Trinosophia and the Egyptian Book of the Dead, since the mystical words the deceased pronounces give him the power he needs to progress. The transmutation of the initiate begins before physical death, via acquisition of this knowledge. The initiate in ancient Egypt was encouraged to gain insight into the spirit realms by developing clairvoyance and practising a state of constant self-awareness. Once he had attained spiritual perception, the true import of the sacred script became revealed to him, and he would begin to develop the faculties required to pass each stage of the trial.

There are strong parallels here with the threefold attributes of freemasonry, which A.E. Waite described as the ethic of life, religious duty and mystical death[23]. In truth, along with all hidden mysteries in the Secret Tradition – masonic or otherwise – both the Trinosophia and The Book of the Dead reveal that inner knowledge is not so very different from ordinary knowledge, once the barriers are removed, and with the practice of humility. The cultivation of the desire to learn is critical. In both The Egyptian Book of the Dead and The Most Holy Trinosophia, a particular system of occult writing is unveiled, each revealing the secret teachings for those for whom they are (at least superficially) intended. Nonetheless, the most important attribute of all is right intention.

---

[23] *The Secret Tradition in Freemasonry*, Waite, A.E., London 1911.

The question arises as to whether the Trinosophia was intended for a readership beyond the confines of the secret society for which it was written *quae in faciem?* Indeed, in the same way that the sojourners in the Holy Royal Arch uncover the Sacred Name, so too is that which is hidden both inexpressible but ultimately discoverable. There is therefore a deeper level of knowledge in the Trinosophia transcending the limited confine of esoteric freemasonry which, like The Egyptian Book of the Dead, conveys the secrets of a successful passage through the afterlife to anyone prepared to make a study of its secrets.

Thoth

Khu (Being of Light) was the name given to the African ibis bird that once lived in Egypt. The ibis represented Djhuty (known to the Graeco-Egyptians as Thoth) the god of judgement, wisdom and knowledge.[24] The Greeks also equated Thoth with Hermes, herald of the gods, and the entire Hermetic tradition owes its origins to this ancient connection. Indeed, the bearer of knowledge was Hermes Trismegistus (Hermes the Thrice-Great) who was understood to be a composite of both gods. Concealed within the text of the Emerald Tablet of Hermes Trismegistus (composed at some point between AD 200-800) is the *credo* of a far more ancient tradition which influenced later Hermeticism.

Not only was Thoth the Being of Light, but he was also known as the god of the dead. The Book of the Dead depicts Thoth as an ibis-headed human, guiding the

---

[24] Djhuty is better known as Thoth (which translates as: "*he who is like the Ibis*").

human soul through the good and bad experiences encountered after death. It was Thoth who judged Horus and Set in the cosmic battle between good and evil, a task that he alone could accomplish as the self-created god of harmony and balance. As such he was often portrayed as a lunar deity, the god of both the dark and light sides of the Moon, and he therefore also plays a prominent role in the final judgement of the soul in the halls of Ausar:

"I am Djhuty, the Perfect Scribe, whose hands are pure, who opposes every evil deed and who records and who erases every wrong, He who is the writing reed of the inviolate God, the Lord of Laws, whose words are written and whose words have dominion over the two worlds. I am the Lord of Justice, the witness of right before the gods. I direct the words to exalt the wronged. I have cast away darkness and driven away the storm." Hymn of Djhuty in the Book of the Dead

The black and white plumage of the African ibis perfectly reflects Thoth's dual role. The Egyptians also associated the black and white ibis with the *ba*[25] (personality soul) of the individual intellect or mind of man. The hieroglyph of a crested ibis on a perch was pronounced *ba-hi,* and the symbolic use of the bird in the Trinosophia is not unsurprisingly figurative of God's gift of wisdom and immortality. At the Serapeum in Hermopolis more than one and a half million

---

[25] Which, following death, would "go forth by day" from its tomb into the world to return at night to the higher realms.

mummified ibises have been discovered. Like the Apis bull, the ibis was believed to contain the immortal essence of the divinity it symbolised on earth. It is believed some eight million birds were mummified in all, each signalling an individual's path to the afterlife. The mummified ibis represented balance in the form of the transcendent divinity ensouled within the material elements, and as such was essentially regarded as an incarnation of Thoth in animal form.

The interred ibises guaranteed Thoth would return to guide the dead. The rooms and palaces we encounter in The Most Holy Trinosophia are allegories of the chambers or halls located in the vast necropolis at the Hermopolis Serapeum, representing as they do the lofty portals between worlds. It is in these spaces that the immortal soul of the aspirant in the Trinosophia contemplates and learns to distinguish the essential from the inessential on his progress through Duat.

Thoth, represented as the god of the moon (harmony) and knowledge.

The Sacred Ibis

Essentially the cosmological system of the ancient Egyptians was that of "mind over matter". This was a result of the material universe being created out of the primal chaos (*Nun*)[26], and therefore the physical realm resided under the Creator's influence. It is believed that both operative and spiritual alchemy arose in Egypt out of attempts to manipulate the Creator's influence on the material world. Developing the power of clairvoyance, understood to be inherent in all people was a key objective of this process, since this concerned itself with developing techniques to communicate with the Divinity lying beyond the transitory appearances of the material world.

---

[26] The *prima materia* of alchemy

Ma'at

As the god of cosmic balance and harmony, Thoth was accompanied by his wife, Ma'at[27]. Like her husband, she was concerned with harmony and justice, and the feather of truth on her head was used to weigh the soul's heart in the judgement halls of Ausar. A trinity was completed with the addition of the goddess Seshat, the daughter of Thoth. Seshat was the patron deity of architects and credited with the invention of writing. She was portrayed holding a wand or reed, with a star above her head representing the astral embodiment of the soul. It is this star which the narrator of the Trinosophia follows in the second section, pursuing his Higher-Self under Thoth's watchful guidance.

---

[27] Ma'at was the daughter of Ra, the deity symbolising the Higher Self in man.

The half-naked woman holding the wand associated with Isis[28] by Manly P. Hall, could instead be an allusion to Seshat. This is because her role was to awaken the initiate to the Higher-Self concealed within the physical senses or architecture of the body. If so, then Seshat is seen here as the bestower of wisdom, blessing the narrator as a scribe at the beginning of his journey through Duat. The mysterious writer of the Trinosophia is associating himself with that object: in other words, he is presenting the potentiality of his Higher Self standing before the patron deity of knowledge and wisdom. Thoth's role was, after all, that of restoring balance by recalling the soul to knowledge of its original, spiritual memory after physical death. This lies at the heart of the Hermetic tradition. The image therefore represents the human soul which has lost all memory of itself, devoid of all self-knowledge and wisdom. The soul stands naked before Seshat, the patron deity of scribes. Here the Trinosophia parallels The Book of the Dead, since both describe the successful path of ascent from the place of our physical encampment on earth to the celestial realms above. This is symbolised in the manuscript by the union of Ma'at with Thoth in the twelfth plate.[29]

---

[28] The sister-wife of Osiris.
[29] Manly P. Hall suggests that as this is in the astrological operation of Pisces, it represents the end of the present Aquarian age and present cycle of history.

Second section illustration
Photo Médiathèque Jacques-Chirac, Troyes Champagne Métropole

Seshat crowned by a star and holding the scribal reed

Thoth and Seshat

The Gateway

"After this I beheld the secrets of the heavens and of paradise, according to its divisions; and of human action, as they weigh it there in balance. I saw the habitations of the elect, and the habitations of the holy..."[30] 1 Enoch

The first illustration we encounter in the fifth section incorporates the Egyptian Sun Disk, which is a symbol of Ra, the guide who grasps the narrator by the hair and lifts him beyond the stars. This is a very powerful image, and one that is recognisable to most:

---

[30] 1 Enoch 41:1

Illustration in The Most Holy Trinosophia
Photo Médiathèque Jacques-Chirac, Troyes Champagne Métropole

The Egyptian Sun Disk

The invisible guide leads the initiate to an immense height across space. The guide does not really abandon the narrator when he falls, it simply *feels* that way to him. He is collected by the guide before any harm occurs and is taken upwards to an immeasurable distance, where he sleeps in death for an indeterminate period. The invisible guide is God in the form of Ra. It is he who in Egyptian cosmology travels with the deceased "across the sky" before judgment. In the following sixth section, the importance of the keys required to open the gateway leading from the underworld to eternal perfection is explained to the narrator by the entity accompanying him:

"My son, you let the opportunity slip away. You could at that moment have grasped the bird, the torch and the altar, you would have become the altar, bird and torch. Now, to reach the most secret place and sublime palace of science, you must go through all the tests."

The narrator has already passed through the three classical stages of Hermetic schooling, namely preparation, illumination, and initiation. We realise that he has successfully negotiated the difficult halls of Ausar, represented by the four elemental trials.[31] The four inscriptions surrounding the images are a cryptic amalgamation of alchemical, hieroglyphic, Hebrew letters and symbols alluding to the gateway or entrance to the Higher Realm through which the narrator is now permitted to pass. As such, he has already acquired the knowledge required to transmute his essence or individualised soul (*ka*) into the immortal life of everlasting spirit. The author of The Most Holy Trinosophia makes no secret of the fact that it is in the fifth section (describing the self-initiate's journey through the astrological sign of Leo) that this perfect knowledge may be acquired to complete the Quest.

That said, the frontispiece or title illustration contains important keys for interpreting the manuscript, since the panels allude to each of the twelve corresponding sections of the manuscript. The reader will observe that on the

---

[31] The narrator has traversed earth from the depths of the dark passageway; the trial of fire in the square chamber; crossed water through the lake; and the trial of air when he struck the neck of the fiery serpent and was drawn up by his invisible guide into the Hall of Wisdom.

frontispiece ten of the twelve panels around the title make up two vertical columns. That on the left contains entirely Egyptian motifs, whereas that on the right contains an eclectic mix of esoteric symbols highlighting the acquisition of knowledge through initiation. One of them is the Egyptian Sun Disk.

Photos Médiathèque Jacques-Chirac, Troyes Champagne Métropole

Photos Médiathèque Jacques-Chirac, Troyes Champagne Métropole

The centre top and bottom panels illustrate the opposites of life and wisdom with death and ignorance. However, they also reflect the four panels in section five of the manuscript, both in their positioning and the importance of their content. Let us consider these analogies a little further. The middle panel at the bottom is left intentionally blank to represent a tomb or the absence of knowledge; whereas the corresponding top panel symbolises God and the acquisition of eternal life and wisdom. The matching inscriptions of ciphers in section five, according to Hall, read as "to the strong is given the burden" and "kindle a fire upon the high place, that the sacrifice may be borne upward to the Desired One."

The corresponding horizontal inscriptions in the fifth section

Hall expands on these by explaining that this is alchemical symbolism drawn from the sanctuary of the Jerusalem Temple. He appears to have missed the direct parallels between these panels and those on the frontispiece, which serve as an additional key to unlocking the full meaning of section five – and therefore the entire book. In essence, the top panel on the frontispiece is a stylised version of the unified altar, bird and torch as the Perfected Mind; and the corresponding blank panel below it represents the narrator at the beginning of his journey who has lost all knowledge of self. These two plates allegorise the third pillar or Middle Path in the Secret Tradition, the unification of opposites, and the direct means of ascending from ignorance to knowledge of the true, inner Self.

The reader may recognize a symbiosis not only with the Book of the Dead, but on a closer reflection of the text with the symbolism in the apocryphal books of Enoch. These provide further – hidden – keys to unlocking the Trinosophia's mysteries. We can only hint at these here and must leave it to the ardent follower to continue his or her own studies. For instance, there may be a direct parallel here with the myth of the two "Enochian Pillars." The first century historian Josephus ascribed to Enoch a tradition that the descendants of Seth, the third son of Adam, prevented the loss of knowledge in the deluge of Noah's Flood by erecting two columns:

> " ...one of brick and the other of stone, and inscribed these discoveries on both; so that, if the pillar of brick disappeared in the deluge, that of stone would remain to teach men what was graven thereon and to inform them that they had also erected one of brick."[32]

The reinvention of writing is credited to the scribes who discovered the knowledge of it on the surviving stone pillar. The importance of these scribes to the ancients

---

[32] Josephus, *Jewish Antiquities* tr. Thackeray, H.S.J., London 1967, 4.33.

cannot be over emphasised, and the reader's attention is drawn to the panel on the left pillar of the frontispiece, which appears to preserve knowledge of the custom of venerating scribes by sitting them beside God, shown here in the form of Thoth as an ibis.

The Scribe
Photos Médiathèque Jacques-Chirac, Troyes Champagne Métropole

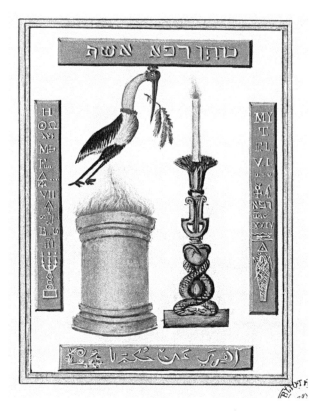

Photo Médiathèque Jacques-Chirac, Troyes Champagne Métropole

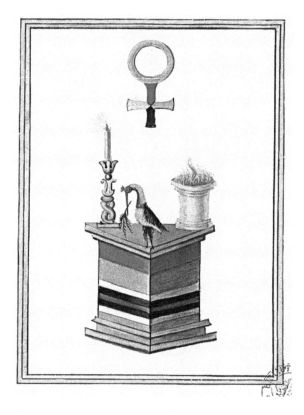

Photo Médiathèque Jacques-Chirac, Troyes Champagne Métropole

44

The Three Wisdoms

The narrator awakens to conscious life in a blissful state in a place identified as the Palace of Wisdom. Close by is the Triangular Altar, an allusion to The Triangular Book of Saint-Germain, upon which is placed a golden altar with a flame burning without source; a lighted torch; and a flightless bird hovering above the immortal flame with a branch in its beak. The true meaning of these images are revealed to us in the sixth section:

> *"The altar, the bird and the torch are the symbols of everything, nothing can be done without them - they themselves are all that is good and great."*

The importance of these words cannot be emphasised enough. The combined image contains the critical symbols for *everything*, and *nothing* can be achieved without them. The first key we encounter is that symbolised by the golden altar. The altar (*Hallaj* in the fifth section, *Athanor* in the following) is not what it appears to be. It is *both* an altar *and* an oven. Knowledge of its correct names grants the narrator power over its dual functions. The altar is symbolic of the foundry oven or fire by which the alchemists of ancient Egypt strove to perfect the elemental world.[33] Graeco-Egyptian alchemy was intimately connected with the assaying of gold, which is the material of the altar:

---

[33] In later sections it is re-designated "Athanor".

"It was the encounter with the symbolisms, myths and techniques of the miners, smelters and smiths which probably gave rise to the first alchemical operations. But above all it was the experimental discovery of the living Substance, such as it was felt by the artisans, which must have played the decisive role."[34] Mercia Eliade, *The Forge and the Crucible*

The Golden Altar
Photo Médiathèque Jacques-Chirac, Troyes Champagne Métropole

The eternal flame atop the golden altar symbolises the Living Substance of God. This is the ever-living material or *ousia* of the Divine within elemental nature. The altar is emblematic of the Burning Bush at the foot of Mount Horeb in the Wilderness of Sinai. The bush was not consumed in flames because it was never in a physical fire, but amidst the Living Substance of God himself. The ibis hovering above the flame is not consumed by the fire either, for the same reason.[35] There is a similar encounter mentioned in the Book of Daniel:

---

[34] *The Forge and the Crucible*, Eliade, M., Chicago 1978 ed., p.148.
[35] Exodus 3:1 – 4:17.

"Then Nebuchadnezzar the king was astonished, and rose up in haste, and spake, and said unto his counsellors, Did not we cast three men bound into the midst of the fire? They answered and said unto the king, True, O king. "Look!" he answered, "I see four men loose, walking in the midst of the fire; and they are not hurt, and the form of the fourth is like the Son of God."

Daniel 3: 24-25

The assaying of gold in ovens was a petition to God, an attempt to encounter the Divinity. The furnace into which Daniel is thrown, the Burning Bush of Exodus and the ovens of the ancient of alchemists are essentially the same thing: portals through which the Divine communicates and presents himself to the seer:

"Know that this primal matter always exists in the hands of the Elect of God and that, in order to obtain it, it does not suffice to be great, rich or powerful; but as I have already told you, it is absolutely necessary to be loved and protected by God." Cagliostro, *The Ritual of Egyptian Freemasonry*[36]

It must be recalled that, except for the Triangular Altar representing the sustaining Creator, the symbols merge in the twelfth and final section of the book to form one integrated body:

---

[36] *The Masonic Magician: The Life and Death of Count Cagliostro and his Egyptian Rite*, Faulks, P. and Cooper, R.l.D., Watkins London 2017, p. 209.

"I crossed the square and, ascending a marble staircase in front of me, saw with astonishment that I had re-entered the hall of the thrones (the first where I found myself when I arrived at the palace of wisdom). The Triangular Altar was still in the centre of this room, but the bird, the altar and the flame were united and formed only one body."

This metaphor is that of the immortal soul (minor spirit) once trapped within physical matter regaining its freedom. In the mid-sections of the manuscript, sections five and six, the narrator's soul has been guided through the physical trials, which motif is now made apparent in the twin columns containing the ciphers flanking the image of the altar, bird and torch. This may also allude to the mystical number eleven within the Martinist tradition, symbolising the incompatibility of physical and spiritual matter:

"The goat burns out of the camp the decomposition of our material form, and also that of the purification of the wicked in the horrible suffering of 56. There is only the spiritual that cleanses and strengthens and vivifies us."[37]

Look carefully at the left cipher and you will see the prominence of the menorah. This was one of the ten vessels of the Tabernacle at the Jerusalem Temple[38], symbolising the seven days of creation and the Light of God. On the opposite

---

[37] *The Lessons of Lyons*, Osborne, M.R., Clink Street, London, p.84 quoting Louis-Claude de Saint-Martin.
[38] The Menorah, the Table, the Altar, the washbasin and Jug, the Ark and the Curtain, the two cherubs and all in its weight.

cipher is the image of physical death, a mummified Egyptian body, wherein the soul returns at night. The twin ciphers are emblematic of the kabbalistic paths of mercy and judgement. The importance of the imagery in the fifth illustration cannot long allude us. The astrological influence is that of Leo, corresponding with the symbolic opposites of strength/weakness, and fire/water. Leo is ruled in the day by the Aten and at night by Osiris. These twin ciphers in the illustration are allegories of the pillars of fire and cloud in the Wilderness, i.e. the material world, symbolised by Egypt.

Moses and the Burning Bush by William Blake

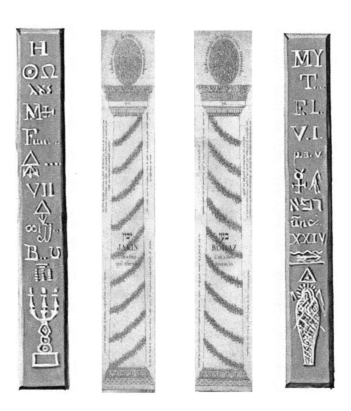

The ciphers representing the twin pillars, Jachin and Boaz
Photo Médiathèque Jacques-Chirac, Troyes Champagne Métropole

The ciphers correspond with the contrasting themes of light and dark, life and death, wisdom and ignorance, and so on. Whilst presented as opposites, there is a much deeper interpretation in the unity of the columns since they merely reflect the different functions of God in this life and in the next. There is in truth one pillar of both fire and cloud in the Biblical narrative, albeit there appears to be two:

"*And the angel of God, which went before the camp of Israel, removed and went behind them; and the pillar of the cloud went from before their face, and stood behind them: and it came between the camp of the Egyptians and the camp of Israel; and it was a cloud and darkness to them, but it gave light by night to these: so that the one came not near the other all the night."*

Exodus 14:19-20

We can see how the column of fire guiding the soul by night (allegorised as the Hebrews) shifts its position to become the column of cloud giving its protection by day. In between these columns is the Middle Path. During the day, therefore, the pillar is merely perceived as a separate pillar of cloud, but at night as fire. This reflects what the Trinosophia has to tell us about the unification of the altar, bird and torch:

"... *opening a door which is between two pillars, [I] found myself in a large hall* [the Palace of Wisdom]"

"... *the bird, the altar and the flame were united and formed only one body."*

Essentially, the narrator is reminding us of the ancient maxim *est una sola res* (there is only one thing) as he passes between the two pillars representing the opposing kabbalistic forces of order and chaos, judgement, and mercy etc. The narrator is free to enter the gate that opens onto the Middle Path leading straight to Kether, the Crown. Just as the Hebrews allegorically passed along the path opened between the parted waves of the Red Sea, so the narrator now stands at his own embarkation point. This duality between slavery and freedom is likened by the narrator to a Palace of Mirrors, reflecting the pure light of Binah and Chokhma. These are now represented in a state of timeless harmony and balance

51

sustained by God, who is represented by the Triangular Altar. Another way of looking at this is to see in these images the perfect allegory for Thoth, Ma'at and Seshat the triune gods of self-knowledge, higher wisdom and harmony.

The final illustration of the fifth section gives us further insight into what is intended by this perfect, mystical union of opposites. In it we see the image of a cloud representing the Divinity, or Divine Substance, enclosing the Seal of Solomon. This equates with the substance or 'stuff' of which God is comprised, the spiritual matter beyond any human comprehension. It is likened to the element of air, which in the Book of the Dead is associated with the Egyptian god Shu. Shu also happens to be the god of lions and the constellation of Leo, and his role was to assist Osiris judge the dead and balance the corresponding spiritual realm with earth. Indeed, a common image of Shu sees him supporting heaven from the earth, joining them together in a procreative union, symbolic of balance and fecundity.

In that sense he is a god of balance, like Thoth. In the Christian tradition the opposites of material and spirit matter have been harmonised only once in history, in the incarnation of the divine consciousness in Christ. As with the two pillars of light and cloud which are really one pillar perceived differently, so too is Christ moved from the position of the pillar of light in his earthly incarnation, to that of the protective pillar of cloud in his resurrection and ascension.

This sets the scene for what is to follow in the remaining sections of the Trinosophia, but the combined image of the fifth illustration (taken as a whole) symbolises man's *reintegration* with the Divine. The perfected work of alchemy is shown here, and its outcome is demonstrated in the twelfth and final section of the manuscript.

Shu supporting the heavens in the regenerative posture

Final illustration of the fifth section
Photo Médiathèque Jacques-Chirac, Troyes Champagne Métropole

The second key to the Gateway is symbolised by the torch (*Majûsî-Mazdéen*), which represents the indwelling Light of God (the Divine Light or *Shekinah*). In kabbalistic terms the torch also symbolises the divine form or soul within man, comprised of the four letters of the Tetragrammaton. The Divine Name therefore *lives* in each human soul:

"You light a lamp for me. YHWH, my God, lights up my darkness." Psalm 18:28

The Torch
Photo Médiathèque Jacques-Chirac, Troyes Champagne Métropole

The lamp also alludes to the golden lampstand located within the tabernacle in the Jerusalem Temple. The reconciliation of these dual forces is mirrored in the torch, where the double snake entwines itself at the base of the ornament, reminiscent of the *Nehushtan* or brazen serpent affixed to a staff which protected the Hebrews from the fiery serpents sent to punish them. The Nehushtan was also for some time placed in the Jerusalem Temple, prior to its removal and destruction by Hezekiah (715 BC - 686 BC).

> *"And the LORD sent fiery serpents among the people, and they bit the people; and much people of Israel died. Therefore the people came to Moses, and said, we have sinned, for we have spoken against the LORD, and against thee; pray unto the LORD, that he take away the serpents from us. And Moses prayed for the people. And the LORD said unto Moses, make thee a fiery serpent, and set it upon a pole; and it shall come to pass, that every one that is bitten, when he looketh upon it, shall live. And Moses made a serpent of brass, and set it upon a pole, and it came to pass, that if a serpent had bitten any man when he beheld the serpent of brass, he lived."*
>
> 2 Numbers 21: 6-8

The Nehushtan is a most singular allegory, the most important of which is its protective and healing powers. The bronze or copper material of its composition alludes to the metallurgical and alchemical processes devised in its construction, both mental and physical. In ancient Egypt, serpents were common symbols for life and healing. On a superficial level the Nehushtan is another version of the *uraei* or snake on the headdress worn by the Pharaohs for the people's protection and wellbeing. However, the healing serpent of Moses is entwined around the staff or crozier given to Moses by God. Unlike Aaron's serpent which is devoured, Moses' serpent is not destroyed but prevails, because its power is derived directly from God. By affixing the brazen serpent to his staff, Moses harmonised these manifest powers with the Divine Mind behind the symbol.

The Uraei

Moses and the Brazen Serpent by William Blake

As we know, the bird in the image (*Aspirma)* is the sacred ibis, corresponding with the immortal phoenix that we see in the final section of the Trinosophia. This is the third symbolic key. The ibis appears here in the colours of the various stages of alchemical transformation, and in so doing contrasts with the opposing black and white plumage of the natural animal. The bird is encountered again by the narrator in the following section when he rues not having taken hold of it earlier. Its central importance is emphasised by its reappearance in the penultimate section of the manuscript. Here the narrator has to work much, much harder to pursue and then nail down the bird in order to claim its powers.

The Bird
Photo Médiathèque Jacques-Chirac, Troyes Champagne Métropole

What appears an oddity, a flightless bird hovering over the eternal flame, is a representation of the Burning Bush, and represents the light, power and presence of God. We will recall that the ibis was emblematic of the mind and intellect of man in ancient Egypt. This part of man's soul, the *Ba*, was individualised and had to be judged for its earthly actions. In the image before us, the narrator is the *Ba*, which, having been judged and found worthy of entering the gate or portal immediate to it, can elect for reintegration and eternal life. The *Ba* of the narrator is too attached to its individuality, and does not comprehend the opportunity it has been given to complete its journey by entering the narrow gate.

The branch in the beak of the ibis is named for a reason (*Hakim*). This is a kabbalistic symbol representing the last of the four gates left open for man's return to Paradise. This was spared the waters of the Great Flood on account of its purity. The branch therefore signifies humanity's return to Eden and the restoration of our original powers there.

The Branch
Photo Médiathèque Jacques-Chirac, Troyes Champagne Métropole

"And the dove came to him in the evening; and, lo, in her mouth was an olive leaf plucked off: so Noah knew that the waters were abated from off the earth." Genesis, 8:11

This ties in with the hieroglyphs reminding us that the Gate or Entranceway is already available to us. Commanding the name of the branch endows authority over Eden, the universe and time. The branch is reminiscent of the ritual food placed in the beak of mummified ibises by the ancient Egyptians, to sustain the soul's journey through the afterlife. Knowledge of the name gives the narrator (the *ba*) power, reflected in the translated meaning of the cipher "to be given the life".

The Triangular Altar on which the forms rest symbolise the Threefold wisdom of Hermes-Trismegistus. The integration of knowledge, imagination and reason culminate in the acquisition of perfect wisdom. A quaternary unity is accomplished with the addition of the Triangular Altar, upon which humanity is reconciled with God and reacquires the original powers lost by Adam at the Fall. The Triangular Altar is that upon which the "everything" of the Golden Altar, Bird and Torch we encounter in the fifth section of the Trinosophia are placed, and is representative of the Divine attributes of Thought, Will and Action. Contained therein is the fourth, or quaternary, aspect of the Divinity, the *outcome* of all these attributes acting in concert. It is worth reflecting on the text of the Emerald Tablet of Hermes Trismegistus in full:

> "*'Tis true without lying, certain and most true. That which is below is like that which is above and that which is above is like that which is below to do the miracle of one only thing and as all things have been and arose from*

one by the mediation of one: so, all things have their birth from this one thing by adaptation. The Sun is its father, the moon its mother, the wind hath carried it in its belly, the earth is its nurse. The father of all perfection in the whole world is here. Its force or power is entire if it be converted into earth. Separate thou the earth from the fire, the subtle from the gross sweetly with great industry. It ascends from the earth to the heaven and again it descends to the earth and receives the force of things superior and inferior. By this means you shall have the glory of the whole world and thereby all obscurity shall fly from you. Its force is above all force, for it vanquishes every subtle thing and penetrates every solid thing. So was the world created. From this are and do come admirable adaptations whereof the means is here in this. Hence, I am called Hermes Trismegistus, having the three parts of the philosophy of the whole world. That which I have said of the operation of the Sun is accomplished and ended."[39]

We are given a picture of the threefold union in *khet* (the physical body), *ba* (the mind) and *ka* (the life force) by operation of the Creator. Hermes' stages of preparation have been completed and, like the narrator in the fifth section, there will be no further physical trials to be faced by him. His time on the material plane is done, and he will not be returning here. By desiring and taking hold, (i.e. desiring to understand) the narrator is in the position to perfect his self-knowledge because he *already* knows everything there is to learn. He holds the

---

[39] Isaac Newton's translation.

Active Key. Just as, in his first four words, the masonic initiate states "I am ... In God." The consequence of the narrator failing to grasp the significance of the threefold images results in him being unable to immediately return to the Palace of Wisdom. Although now designated a "wise-man"[40] by the spirit guides, he has to continue on his journey to regain that which he has failed to understand.

Photo Médiathèque Jacques-Chirac, Troyes Champagne Métropole

Nevertheless, the narrator is given help in the form of eight gifts, each with the powers he needs to help him through the higher spirit realms through which he must pass. He must however use these in the correct order and not take any short cuts, as they must be used consecutively. These gifts represent the burial goods found in ancient Egyptian tombs, to guide and support the deceased. The crystal cup containing a brilliant saffron liquor of exquisite fragrance alludes to the Egyptian belief that the *ka* was sustained by food and drink: *"Finish this beverage. It will be the only food you will take during your journey."*

---

[40] Shaman.

A Book of the Dead

The perfected or fully integrated soul enters Heaven in the twelfth and final section of the Trinosophia. The image presented to us corresponds with the culmination of the four component parts of the deceased's passage into the Field of Reeds as described in the Book of the Dead, namely:

- absolution;

- the perfection of wisdom;

- the resurrected body; and

- eternal life

The image of the man and the woman in the twelfth section alludes to the marriage of Thoth and Ma'at. As such, Thoth is shown in both masculine and feminine aspects, standing above a new earth amidst the Divine *ousia*[41] emanating from the *lapis philosophorum* representing eternal life. This imagery depicts the journey's end in the final astrological cycle of Pisces. The image is rich, resplendent, beautiful, and harkens back to the image of the seal of Solomon enclosed in the *ousia* representing the substance of God in the fifth section.

The authorship of The Most Holy Trinosophia may elude us, but we can be certain that whoever wrote the manuscript had a complete understanding of

---

[41] Greek, οὐσία.

ancient Egyptian cosmogony. The Most Holy Trinosophia is not an initiatory manual from a long extinct masonic order: it is an abridged Book of the Dead. More accurately, it is a Book *for* the Dead. Like its Egyptian counterpart, the manuscript deals with the theme of the soul approaching death and passing through the trials of the underworld on its journey to immortality.

Twelfth section illustration
Photo Médiathèque Jacques-Chirac, Troyes Champagne Métropole

Therein is contained the mystery of the sacred *via media* or Red Sea passage leading to enlightenment, amid the trials of this world and the worlds to come. The message is simple enough: prepare for death and contemplate acquiring a true understanding through building a temple or structure of your own wisdom.

In parting let us consider the words of A. E. Waite, who passed into the spirit nearly eighty years ago:

"There only remains the Mind of Man, excogitating and incogitating, conceiving and dwelling on aspects of the Mind of God, and setting forth its own travels therein. My thesis is, that all whatsoever which we know, shall and can know of God, lies within these measures – the measures of the human Mind."[42]

Est una sola res.

M. R. Osborne, M.A.
Northampton, August 2021

---

[42] *Shadows of Life and Thought: A Retrospective Review in the Form of Memoirs,* Waite, A. E., London,1938 p. 237.

THE MOST HOLY TRINOSOPHIA

otherwise known as

THE MOST HOLY THREEFOLD

WISDOM

The front cover
Photo Médiathèque Jacques-Chirac, Troyes Champagne Métropole

The spine and the fore-edge
Photo Médiathèque Jacques-Chirac, Troyes Champagne Métropole

67

The Top-edge
Photo Médiathèque Jacques-Chirac, Troyes Champagne Métropole

The Bottom-edge
Photo Médiathèque Jacques-Chirac, Troyes Champagne Métropole

The back cover
Photo Médiathèque Jacques-Chirac, Troyes Champagne Métropole

Ce Manuscrit est la seule copie existante de la fameuse Trismégistie du C.te De St Germain, qu'il détruisit lui même dans un dernier voyage.

J.B. C. Philotaume

The Inside Flysheet

LA

TRINOSOPHIE

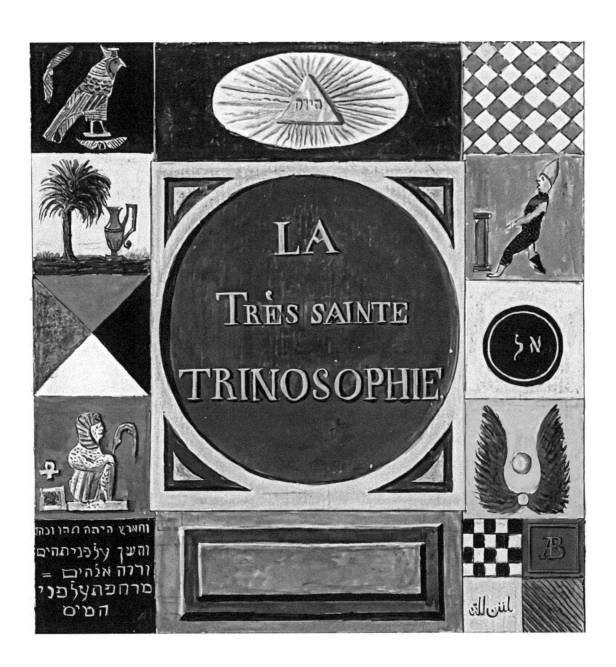

Photo Médiathèque Jacques-Chirac, Troyes Champagne Métropole

C'est dans l'azile des criminels
dans les cachots de L'Inquisition, que
votre ami trace ces lignes qui doivent
servir à votre instruction. En songeant
aux aux avantages inapréciables que doit
jvous, vous procurer ces écrits de l'amitié, Je

sans s'adoucir les horreurs d'une captivité
aussi longue que peu méritée... j'ai du
plaisir à penser qu'environné de-
gardes, chargé de fers, un esclave peut
encore élever son ami au dessus des -
puissants, des monarques qui gouvernent
ces lieu d'éxil.

Vous allez pénétrer mon chèr
Philochale dans le sanctuaire des -
sciences sublimes; ma main va lever
pour vous le voile impénétrable qui
dérobe aux yeux du vulguaire, le
tabernacle, le sanctuaire ou l'éternel
déposa les secrets de la nature, secrets
qu'il réserve pour quelquéśetres privilé-
-giés, pour les Elus que sa toute puis-

sance créa pour Voir pour planer à
sa suite dans l'immensité de sa Gloire,
et détourner sur l'espèce humaine un
des Rayons qui brillent au tour de
son Throne d'or . ——

Puisse l'exemple de votre ami.
être pour vous une leçon salutaire et
je bénirai les longues années d'épreuves
que les méchans m'ont fait subir . —

Deux écueuils également
dangereux. se présenteront sans cesse sur
vos pas l'un outragerois les droits sacrés
de chaque individu c'est L'Abus du
pouvoir que DIEU vous auroit confié,
l'autre causerois votre perte c'est
L'Indiscretion …. tous deux sont nés

Photo Médiathèque Jacques-Chirac, Troyes Champagne Métropole

76

d'une même mere, tous deux doivent
l'existence à l'Orgueil, la foiblesse hu-
_maine les allaita, ils sont aveugles,
leur mère les conduit, par son secours
ces deux Monstres, vont porter leur
soufle impur jusque dans les cœurs
des **Elus** du très haut malheur à
celui qui abuseroit des dons du ciel
pour servir ses passions la main toute
puissante qui lui soumit les Élé_
_mens, le briseroit comme un foible
_ Roseau une éternité de tourmens
pourroit à peine expier son crime
les Esprits Infernaux souriroient
avec dédain aux pleurs de l'être
dont la voix menaçante les fit si_

souvent trembler au sein de leurs
abimes de feu.

Ce n'est pas pour vous
Philochale que j'esquisse ce tableau
effrayant, l'ami de l'humanité ne
deviendra jamais son persécuteur.....
mais l'Indiscretion mon fils ce besoin
impérieux d'inspirer l'étonnement,
l'admiration, voila le précipice que
je redoute pour vous, Dieu laisse
aux hommes le soin de punir le ministre
imprudent qui permet à l'œuil du
Prophâne de pénétrer dans le sanctuai-
-re mystérieux; ô Philochale que mes
malheurs soient sans cesse présens
à votre esprit, & moi aussi j'ai connu

le bonheur, comblé des bienfaits du ciel:
entouré d'une puissance telle que l'enten-
-dement humain ne peut la concevoir
commandant aux génies qui dirigent
le monde, heureux du bonheur que je
faisais naître, je goutais au sein —
d'une famille adorée la félicité que —
l'Éternel accorde à ses enfans chéris...
un instant a tout détruit, j'ai parlé
et tout s'est évanoui comme un —
nuage, ô mon fils ne suivez pas mes
traces .... qu'un vain désir de briller —
aux yeux du monde ne cause pas
aussi votre perte .... pensez à moi, —
c'est dans un cachot, le corps brisé
par les tortures que votre ami vous-
        1r les tortures votre

écrire; Philocale réfléchissez, que la main
qui trace ces caractères porte l'empreinte
des fers qui l'accablent..... Dieu m'a
puni , mais quai-je fais aux homes
cruels qui me persécutent? Quel
droit ont ils pour intéroger le
ministre de l'Éternel? ils me de-
–mandent quelles sont les preuves de
ma mission, mes témoins sont des
prodiges, mes deffenseurs mes vertus,
une vie intacte, un cœur pur, que
dis-je ai-je encore le droit de me
plaindre, j'ai parlé le très haut
m'a livré sans force et sans puissan-
–ce aux fureurs de lavare fanatisme,
le bras qui jadis pouvois renverser –.

Photo Médiathèque Jacques-Chirac, Troyes Champagne Métropole#

une armée, peut à peine aujourd'hui —
soulever les chaines qui l'appesantisse.

Je m'égare, je dois rendre grace —
a l'éternelle Justice... le dieu ven-
-geur à pardonné à son enfant —
repentant un esprit Aërien a —
franchit les murs qui me séparent
du monde; resplendissant de lumi-
-ere, il s'est présenté devant moi
il a fixé le terme de ma captivité, —
dans deux ans mes malheurs finiront
mes bourreaux en entrant dans mon
cachot le trouveront désert en
bientot purifié par les 4 élémens
pur comme le génie du feu je —
reprendrai le rang glorieux ou la.

bonté Divine, ma élevé mais combien
ce terme est encore éloigné combien
deux années paroissent longues à
celui qui les passe dans les souffrances,
dans les humiliations, non contens de
me faire souffrir les suplices les plus
horribles mes persécuteurs ont employé
pour me tourmenter des moyens plus
surs plus odieux encore, ils ont appel-
-lé l'infamie sur ma tête, ils ont fait
de mon nom un objet d'opprobre,
les enfants des hommes reculent
avec effroi quand le hazard les a
faits approcher des murs de ma
prison, ils craignent qu'une vap-
-eur mortelle ne s'échappe par

l'ouverture etroite qui laisse passer
comme a regrets un rayon de lumi
ère dans mon cachot. Ô Philocale
c'est là le coup le plus cruel dont
ils pouvoient m'accabler ....

    J'ignore encore si je pourrai
vous faire parvenir cet ouvrage ...
Je juge des difficultés que j'éprouve
_rai pour le faire sortir de ce lieu de
tourmens, par celles qu'il a fallu
vaincre pour le terminer, privé_
de tous secours j'ai moi même com_
_posé les agens qui m'étaient néces
_saires. Le feu de ma lampe quel
ques pièces de moñaies en peu de
substances chimiques échappées _

aux regards scrutateurs de mes bourreaux.
ont produit les couleurs qui ornent ce
fruit des loisirs d'un prisonnier. —
Profitez, des instructions de votre
malheureux ami. elles sont tellement
claires qu'il seroit a craindre que
ces écrits tombant en d'autres mains
que les votres... souvenez vous seu-
-lement que tout doit vous servir
une ligne mal expliquée un caractere
oublié, vous empêcheroient de lever le
voile que la main du créateur à
posé sur le Sphinx.
Adieu Philocale ne me plai
-gnez pas la clemence de l'Éternel
égale sa justice à la premiere. —

Photo Médiathèque Jacques-Chirac, Troyes Champagne Métropole

84

assemblée mystérieuse, vous reverez
votre ami. Je vous salue en Dieu,
bientôt je donnerai le baiser de
paix à mon frère.

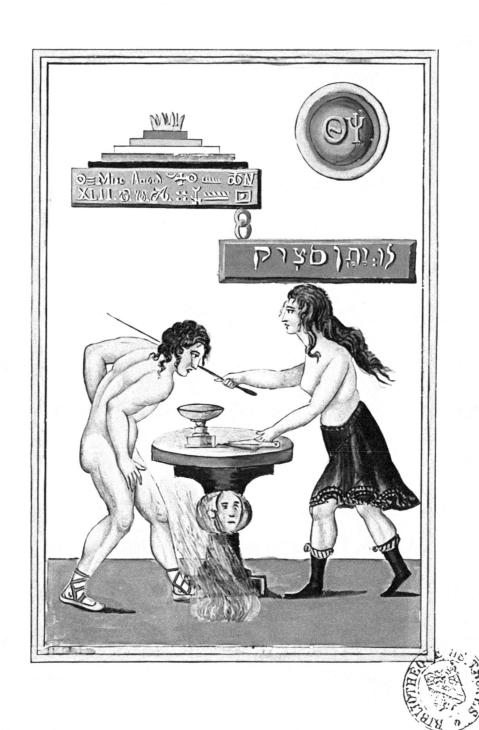

Photo Médiathèque Jacques-Chirac, Troyes Champagne Métropole

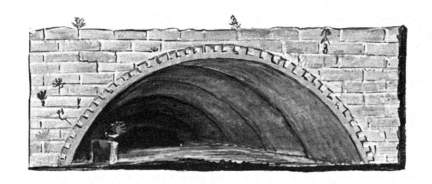

Il étoit nuit, la lune cachée
par des nuages sombres ne jettoit qu'une
lueur incertaine. sur les blocs de lave
qui environnent la Solfatare, la tête
couverte du voile de Lin, tenant dans
mes mains le rameau d'or je m'avançais

Photo Médiathèque Jacques-Chirac, Troyes Champagne Métropole

sans crainte vers le lieu ou j'avois reçu
l'ordre de passer la nuit . Errant
sur un sable brûlant, je le sentois
a chaque instant s'affaisser sous mes
pas les nuages s'ammoncelaient —
sur ma tête, l'éclair sillonnait la
nue, et donnait une teinte sangl-
ante aux flammes du volcan . . . . .
Enfin j'arrive, je trouve un autel —
de fer j'y place le rameau mystérieux . . . . Je prononce les mots redou-
tables . . . . a l'instant la terre tremble,
sous mes pieds le tonnere éclate . . . . .
les mugissements du Vésuve répon-
dent à ces coups redoublés ses —
feux se joignent aux feux de la

foudre.... les cœurs des Génies s'élevant
dans les airs en font répéter aux échos
les louanges du créateur....la branche
consacrée que j'avais placée sur l'autel
triangulaire, s'enflâme tout à coup une
épaisse fumée m'environne, je cesse de
voir, plongé dans les ténèbres je crus
descendre dans un abîme, J'ignore
combien de temps je restai dans cette
situation mais en ouvrant les yeux, je
cherchai vainement les objets qui m'entou-
-raient quelquetems auparavant; l'autel
le Vésuve la campagne de Naples avoient
fui loin de mes yeux j'étois dans un
vaste souterrain, seul, éloigné du monde
entier....près de moi était une robe

longue, blanche, son tissu délié me sembla
composé de fil de lin, sur une masse de
granit était posée une lampe de cuivre
au dessus une table noire chargée de
caractères grecs m'indiquaient la route
que je devois suivre je pris la lampe
et après avoir revêtu la robe je
m'engageai dans un chemin étroit
dont les parois étaient revêtus de marbre
noir.... Il avait trois mille de longueur,
mes pas retentissaient d'une manière
effrayante sous ces voûtes silencieuses
enfin je trouvai une porte elle condui-
sait à des degrés, je les descendis,
après avoir marché longtems je crus
appercevoir une lueur errante devant

moi je cachai ma lampe je fixai mes yeux
sur l'objet que j'entrevoyais il se dissipa
s'évanouit comme une ombre.

Sans reproches sur le passé sans
crainte sur l'avenir je continuai ma
route elle devenait de plus en plus
pénible .... toujours engagé dans des
galeries composées de quartiers de pierres
noires ... je n'osais fixer le terme de
mon voyage souterrain enfin après
une marche immense, j'arrivai à
une place quarrée; une porte souvrait
au milieu de chacune de ses quatre
faces elles étaient de couleur différen-
te et placée chacune à l'un des quatre
points cardinaux, j'entrai par celle.

du Septentrion elle étoit noire, celle qui
me faisoit face étoit rouge, la porte
de l'orient étoit bleue, celle qui lui
étoit opposée étoit d'une blancheur
éclatante ... au centre de cette salle
étoit une masse quarrée, une étoile
de cristal brillant sur son milieu.
on voyoit une peinture sur la face
septentrionale elle représentoit une
femme nue jusqu'à la ceinture, une
draperie noire lui tomboit sur les
genoux deux bandes d'argent
ornaient son vêtement, dans sa
main étoit une baguette, elle la
posoit sur le front d'un homme
placé vis-à-vis d'elle. une table terminée

par un seul pied étais entre eux deux; sur la table étais une coupe et un fer de lance. Une flame soudaine s'élevais de terre. et sembloit se diriger vers l'homme une inscription expliquais le sujet de cette peinture. Une autre m'indiquais les moyens que je devois employer pour sortir de cette salle.

Je voulus me retirer après avoir considéré le tableau et l'étoile. j'allais entrer dans la porte rouge quand tournant sur ses gonds avec un bruit épouvantable elle se refer- ma devant moi, je voulois tenter la même épreuve sur celle que

décorois la couleur du ciel, elle ne se
ferma point mais un bruit soudain
me fit détourner la tête, je vis —
l'étoile sagitter, elle se détache roule
et se plonge rapidement dans —
l'ouverture dela porte blanche, je
la suivis aussitôt.

95

Un vent impétueux s'é
leva, jeus soine a conserver ma
lampe allumée ensin un perron
de marbre blanc s'offrit à ma
vue j'y montai par neuf marches

arrivé `a la derniere, j'apperçus une
immense étendue, d'eau; des torrens
impétueux se faisaient entendre
`a ma droite, `a gauche une pluie
froide mellée de masses de grêle
tombait près de moi je consi-
derais cette scene. majestueuse
quand l'étoile qui m'avait guidé
sur le perron et qui se balançait
lentement sur ma tête se plon-
_gea dans le gouffre je crus lire
les ordres du très haut je me_
precipitai au milieu des vagues
une main invisible saisit ma_
lampe et la posa sur le somet,
de ma tête. Je fendis l'onde_

écumeuse et m'efforçai de gagner le point opposé à celui dont j'étois parti, enfin je vis à l'horison une foible clarté, je me hatai, j'étois au milieu des eaux et la sueur couvroit mon visage, je m'épuisais en vains efforts la rive que je pouvois à peine appercevoir sembloit fuir devant moi à mesure que j'avançais, mes forces m'abandonnaient, je ne craignois pas de mourir, mais de mourir sans être illuminé.. je perdis courage en levant vers la voute mes yeux baignés de pleurs. Je m'écriai « Judica judicium meum et redime me, propter eloquium tuum vivifica me,

`a peine pouvois-je agiter mes membres
fatigués j'enfonçais de plus en plus
quand j'apperçus près de moi une
barque, un homme couvert de riches
habits, la conduisoit, je remarquai
que la proue étoit tournée vers la
rive que j'avois quitté, il s'approcha,
une couronne d'or brillait sur son
front vade me cum me dit-il, me
cum principium in terris, instruam
te in via hac quâ gradueris. Je
lui repondis `a l'instant, bonum
est sperare in domino quam
considere in principibus ..... `a
l'instant la barque, et le monar
que s'abimerent dans le fleuve,

une force nouvelle sembla couler
dans mes veines je parvins à gagner
le but de mes fatigues, je me trouvai
sur un rivage semé de sable vert.
Un mur d'argent étoit devant
moi deux lames de marbre rouge
étaient incrustées dans son épais-
seur, j'approchai, l'une étoit chargé
de caractères sacrés sur l'autre
étoit gravée une ligne de lettres
grecques. entre les deux lames
étoit un cercle de fer deux
lions, l'un rouge et l'autre noir,
reposaient sur des nuages et
semblaient garder une couroñe
d'or placée au dessus deux, on

voyois encore. près du cercle un arc:
et deux flèches je lus quelques —
caracteres écrits sur les flancs d'un
des lions. à peine avait-je observé ces
differens emblêmes, qu'ils disparu—
—rent avec la muraille. qui les —
contenait .

Photo Médiathèque Jacques-Chirac, Troyes Champagne Métropole

102

A sa place un lac de feu se présenta devant moi, le soufre et le bitume roulaient leurs flots enflammés je frémis, une voix éclatante m'ordonna de traverser.

103

ces flâmes, j'obeis en les flammes —
semblerent avoir perdu leur acti-
-vité longtems je marchai au milieu
de l'incendie, arrivé dans un espace
circulaire, je contemplai le pompeux
spectacle dons la bonté du ciel —
daignait me faire jouir.

Quarante colonnes de feu —
décoraient la salle dans laquelle je —
me trouvois un coté des colonnes bril-
-loit d'un feu blanc en vif, l'autre
sembloit dans l'ombre, une flâme
noirâtre le couvrait; au centre de
ce lieu s'élevait un autel en forme
de serpent, un or verd embellissoit
son écaille diaprée sur laquelle se

Photo Médiathèque Jacques-Chirac, Troyes Champagne Métropole

reflettaient les flammes qui l'environ-
naient, ses yeux semblaient des
rubis, une inscription argentée etait
posée près de lui. Une riche épée etait
plantée en terre près du serpent,
une coupe reposoit sur sa tête...

J'entendis le cœur des esprits céles-
tes, une voix me dit le terme de tes
travaux approche, prends le glaive,
frappe le serpent.

De tirai l'épée de son four
reau en m'approchant de l'autel
je pris la coupe d'une main et de
l'autre je portai un coup terrible
sur le col du serpent, l'épée rebon-
dit, le coup raisonna comme si

Photo Médiathèque Jacques-Chirac, Troyes Champagne Métropole

j'avois frappé une cloche d'airain,
à peine avois-je obéi à la voix que
l'autel disparût, les colonnes se per-
-dirent dans l'immensité, le son que
j'avois entendu en frappant l'autel
se répéta comme si mille coups
étaient frappés en même temps,
une main me saisit par les che-
-veux et m'éleva vers la voute, elle
souvrit pour me livrer passage,
des vains fantômes se présentèrent
devant moi, des Hydres, des Lamies
m'entourèrent de serpens, la vue de
l'epée que je tenois à la main écarta
cette foule immonde comme les
premiers rayons du jour dissipent

Photo Médiathèque Jacques-Chirac, Troyes Champagne Métropole

les songes frêles enfans dela nuits.
Après être monté par une ligne
perpendiculaire à travers les
couches qui composent les parrois
du globe. Je revis la lumiere du
Jour.

Photo Médiathèque Jacques-Chirac, Troyes Champagne Métropole

À peine étais-je parvenu à
la surface de la terre, que mon con-
_ducteur invisible m'entraîna plus-
rapidement encore, la vélocité avec
laquelle nous parcourions les _

espaces aériens ne peut être compa-
-rée à rien qu'à elle même; en un
instant j'eus perdu de vue les plai-
-nes sur les qu'elles je dominais —
j'avais observé avec étonnement, que
j'étais sorti du sein de la terre, loin
des campagnes de Naples une —
plaine déserte quelques masses tri-
-angulaires étaient les seuls objets —
que j'eusse apperçu. Bientôt mal-
-gré les épreuves que j'avois subies,
une nouvelle terreur vint m'assaillir;
la terre ne me semblait plus qu'un
nuage confus, j'étois élevé à une
hauteur immense mon guide invi-
-sible m'abandonna je redescendis

pendant un asser long tems. je
roulai dans l'espace ; déja la terre
se deployais a mes regards trou_
_blés . . . je pouvois calculer combien
de minutes se passeraient avans
que j'aille me briser contre un
rocher. Bientoi prompts côme
la pensée mon conducteur se_
précipe après moi il me reprend
m'enleve encore une fois, il me_
laisse retomber, enfin il m'eleve_
avec lui `a une distance incom_
_mensurable, je voyois des globes
rouler autour de moi, des terres
graviter `a mes pieds tous `a_
coup le genie qui me portois

me touche les yeux, je perdis le
sentiment. J'ignore combien de
temps je passai en cet état, à
mon réveil je me trouvai couché
sur un riche coussin; des fleurs
des aromates, embaumaient l'air
que je respirais.... Une robe
bleu semée d'étoiles d'or, avoit
remplacé le vêtement de lin.
vis-à-vis de moi étais un autel
Jaune. un feu pur s'en exhalait
sans qu'aucune autre substance
que l'autel même l'alimentât.
Des caractères noirs étaient
gravés sur sa baze. Auprès
doit un flambeau allumé qui

brilloit comme le soleil, au dessus
etoit un oiseau dont les pieds —
etaient noirs, le corps d'argent;
la tête rouge les ailes noires et
Le Col d'or. Il s'agitait sans
cesse mais sans faire usage de
ses ailes. Il ne pouvoit voler
que lorsqu'il se trouvoit au milieu
des flammes. dans son bec etoit
une branche verte son nom est
 celui de l'autel —
est l'autel, l'oiseau et le
flambeau sont le sïmbole de tout,
rien ne peut être fait sans —
eux, eux même sont tout ce —
qui est bon et grand. le flambeau

Photo Médiathèque Jacques-Chirac, Troyes Champagne Métropole

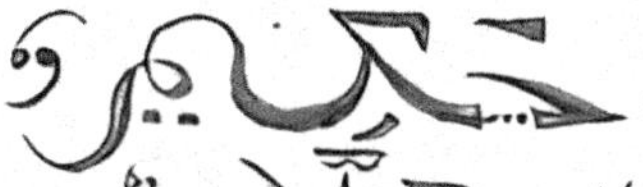

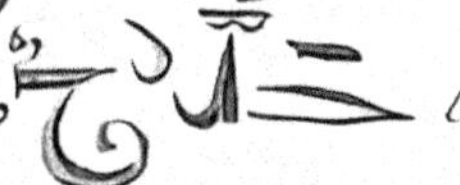

se nomme . مَبَرُزَمي

Quatre inscriptions entou-

-raient ces différents emblêmes.

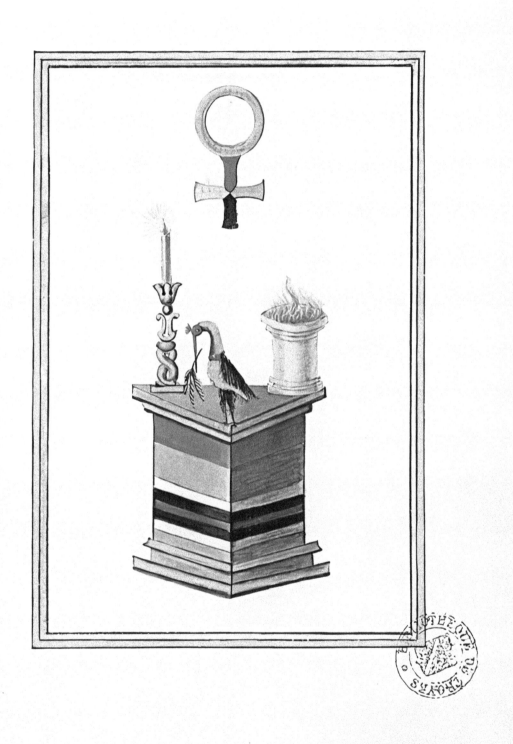

Je me détournai et j'apperçus un palais immense, sa baze re-
-posoit sur des nuages, des marbres
composaient sa masse; sa forme —
étois triangulaire quatre étages de-

colonnes s'élevaient les uns sur les autres.
Une boule dorée terminait cet édifice
le premier rang de colonne étoit blanc,
le second noir. le troisieme verd le der
-nier etoit d'un rouge brillant, je
voulus après avoir admiré cet ou-
-vrage des artistes éternels retourner au
lieu ou étoient l'autel, l'Oiseau et
le flambeau, je voulois encore les
observer ils étoient disparus, je les
cherchois des yeux quand les portes
du palais s'ouvrirent, un vieillard
vénérable en sortit, sa robe etoit
semblable à la mienne excepté
qu'un soleil doré brilloit sur sa
poitrine sa main droite tenoit

Photo Médiathèque Jacques-Chirac, Troyes Champagne Métropole

117

une branche verte, l'autre soutenois
un encensoir, une chaine de bois-
dois attachée `a son col une thiare
pointue ·comme celle de zoroastre
coucrois sa tête blanchie il s'approcha
de moi; le sourire dela bienveillance
erroir sur ses levres,, adore Dieu
me dit-il en langue Persane, c'est
lui qui la soutenu dans les épreuves
son esprit étois avec toi, mon fils
tu as laissé fuir l'occasion tu pou-
-vais `a l'instant saisir l'oiseau
le flambeau et
l'autel tu serois devenu
`a la. fois Autel Oiseau et Flam-
-beau. Il faut `a présent pour-

118

parvenir au lieu le plus secret du
Palais des sciences sublimes que tu
en parcours tous les détours. viens..
Je dois avant tout le présenter à
mes frères. Il me prit la main et
m'introduisit dans une vaste salle.
Des yeux vulgaires ne peuvent
concevoir la forme et la richesse
des ornemens qui l'embellissoient.
trois cens soixante colonnes l'entourai-
-ent de toutes parts, au plafond étoit
une croix rouge, blanche, bleue et
noire. un anneau d'or la soutenoit.
Au centre de la salle étoit un autel
triangulaire composé des quatre
élémens sur ses trois points étaient

posés l'oiseau, l'autel et le flambeau.
Ils ont changé de nom me dit mon
guide, ici on nomme l'oiseau אספיר,
l'autel חמבנא et le flambeau בפדיר;
la salle est appellée. אָכֶ, l'autel
triangulaire ΑΘΑΝΩΡ autour de
l'autel étaient placés quatre-vingt-
-un Thrônes; on montait à chacun
par neuf marches de hauteur inégale;
des housses rouges les couvraient.

Pendant que j'examinois
les thrônes, le son d'une trompette
se fit entendre; à ce bruit, les
portes de la salle אָכֶ tournerent
sur leurs gonds pour laisser passer
soixante dix neuf personnes, toutes

velues comme mon conducteur.
Elles s'approcherent lentement, et
s'assirent sur les thrônes, mon guide
se tint debout auprès de moi. Un
viellard distingué de ses frères par
un manteau de pourpre dont les
bords étaient chargés de caracteres
en broderies, se leva et mon guide
prenant la parole en langue sacré
Voila dit-il un de nos enfans que
Dieu veut rendre aussi grand que
ses peres. Que la volonté du seigne-
-ur s'accomplisse répondit le viellard.
Mon fils ajoutatil en s'adressant à
moi votre temps d'épreuves physiques
est accompli... Il vous reste à faire

de grands voyage, désormais vous vous
appellerez, ٱللَّٮٮ avant de par-
-courir cet édifice, huit de mes frères
et moi allons vous faire, chacun un
present il vint à moi et me doña
avec le baiser de paix. un cûbe de
terre grise on le nomme ﺎﺤﻤ le
second trois cylindres de pierre noire
appelée קבד le troisième un morceau
de cristal arrondi, on l'appele ﺟﻮﺍﺍ
le quatrieme une aigrette de plumes
bleues nommée ﺍﺷﻘﻮﺷﻖ le cinquieme, y
joignit un vase d'argent, qui porte
le nom de נשׁם le sixieme. une grap-
-pe de raisin connue parmi les sa-
-ges sous le nom de מתם רשׁם le septième.

me presenta une figure d'oiseau sembla-
-ble pour la forme `a הַחֹרִי mais il
n'avoit pas ses brillantes couleurs, il
étoit d'argent, il porte le même nom
me dit-il, c'est `a toi a lui donner les
mêmes vertus. le huitième me donna
un petit autel ressemblant, aussi `a l'au-
-tel נִפְרַית enfin mon conducteur me
-mit dans   main un flambeau compo-
-sé comme פֹרוֹת de particules brillan-
-tes mais il étoit éteint. c'est `a toi ajou-
-ta t'il comme ceux qui l'avoient précédé
`a lui donner les mêmes vertus, réfléchis
sur ces dons, me dit ensuite le chef=
des sages tous tendent également `a
la perfection, mais nul n'est parfait.

par lui même, c'est de leur mélange —
que doit sortir l'ouvrage divin. sache
encore que tous sont nuls si tu ne les
emploie suivant l'ordre dans le qu'el
ils t'ont été donné. le second qui sert
a employer le premier ne seroit qu'
une matiere brute sans chaleur, sans
utilité sans le secours de celui qui vient
après lui, garde soigneusement les
présens que tu as reçu. et comencez
les voyages après avoir bû dans la
coupe de vie. Il me présenta dans
une coupe de cristal une liqueur
brillante et safranée son goust étoit
délicieux un parfum exquis s'en éxal
toit. Je voulus rendre la coupe après

avoir trempé mes lèvres dans la liqueur,
achève me dit le vieillard, ce breuvage
sera la seule nouriture que tu prendras
pendant le temps de tes voyages. J'obéis
et je sentis un feu divin parcourir
tous les fibres de mon corps, j'étois plus
forts, plus courageux, mes facultés même
intellectuelles, semblaient être doublées.

Je me hâtai de donner le salut des
sages à l'auguste assemblée que j'allais
quitter, et par les ordres de mon conduc-
-teur, je m'enfonçai dans une longue
galerie qui se trouvoit à ma droite.

A l'entrée de la galerie dans
la qu'elle je me trouvois étoit posée une
cuve d'acier, a mon approche elle se
remplit d'une eau pure come le cris-
-tal, qui vint s'épurer sur un sable. —

blanc en fin la cuve étoit ovale; Elle
étoit soutenue sur trois pieds d'airain.
une lame noire incrustée sur le coté
qui regardoit la porte renfermoit
quelques caractères. près dela cuve
étoit un voile de lin. au dessus d'elle
Deux colonnes de marbre vert suppor-
_toient une plaque de marbre arrondie.
On y voyoit entourée de deux inscrip-
_tions la figure du cachet sacré
formée d'une croix de quatre couleurs,
attachée à une traverse d'or qui sou-
_tient (★) Deux autres cercles concentriques
_ le plus grand, noir. l'autre rouge. à
l'une des colonnes étoit attachée une
hache d'argent, dont la hampe étoit

(★) Deux cercles quatrouroxx

Photo Médiathèque Jacques-Chirac, Troyes Champagne Métropole

bleue elle s'appelle קלנקירוח après avoir
lû les inscriptions, je m'approchai de la
cuve et je m'y lavai, en commençant
par les mains, je finis par m'y plon-
-ger, tout entier. J'y restai trois jours,
en sortant de l'eau je m'apperçus
qu'elle avoit perdu sa transparence.
son sable étoit devenu grisâtre, des
particules couleur de rouille s'agittai-
-ent dans le fluide. Je voulus me
secher avec le secours du voile de lin,
mais de nouvelles gouttes d'eau rem-
-plaçaient sans cesse celles dont le
linge s'imbibait je renonçai à me
sécher avec le voile et me tenant à
l'ombre j'y restai immobile pendant

six jours entiers ; au bout de ce temps la
source de ces eaux fut tarie je me
trouvai sec et plus leger quoique mes
forces me parussent augmentées. après
m'être promené quelque temps je re-
tournai a la Cuve, l'eau quelle con-
-tenoit étoit epuisée, a sa place étoit
une liqueur rougeâtre, le sable étoit
gris et métallique. Je m'y baignai de
nouveau, en observant cependant de
n'y rester que quelques instans, en me
retirant je vis que j'avois absorbé une
partie du liquide. cette fois je ne ten-
-tai pas de tarir avec le linge, la liqu-
-eur dont j'étois imprégné, elle l'au-
-roit détruit à l'instant ; tant elle

dois sortes en corrosive. Je fus à l'autre
bout de la gallerie m'étendre sur un
lit de sable chaud, j'y passai sept jours
au bout de ce temps je revins `a la
cuve l'eau dois semblable a la premi-
-ere, je m'y replongeai et en ressortis
après m'être lavé avec soin. cette fois
je parvins sans peine `a m'essuyer,
enfin après m'être purifié selon
les instructions que j'avois reçu, je
mé disposai `a sortir de cette gale-
_rie après y être resté seize jours.

Je quittai la galerie par une
porte basse et étroite et j'entrai
dans un appartement circulaire
ses lambris étoient de bois de frê-
ne et de sandal. au fond de l'ap-

_partements sur un socle composé
de seps de vigne reposait une
masse de sel blanc et brillant,
au dessus étoit un tableau il représen-
_toit un lion blanc couronné. et
une grappe de raisin, ils étoient
posés sur un même plateau, que
la fumée d'un brasier allumé
élevoit dans les airs. A ma droite
et à ma gauche s'ouvraient deux
portes l'une donnoit sur une
plaine aride. Un vent sec et
brulant y régnoit en tout temps.
L'autre porte s'ouvroit sur un lac
à l'extrémité du quel on apper-
_cevoit une façade de marbre noir.

Je m'approchai près de l'autel
et pris dans mes mains du sel
blanc et brillant que les sages
appellent מרח רשא Je m'en frottai
tout le corps... Je m'en pénétrai et
après avoir lu les hieroglyphes qui
accompagnoient le tableau je
m'apprêtai a quitter cette salle.
mon premier dessein étoit de sortir
par la porte qui donnoit sur la
plaine, mais une vapeur brûlante
s'en exalloit, je préférai le chemin
opposé, j'avois la liberté de choisir,
avec la condition cependant de ne
pas quitter celui que j'aurois pris...
Je me décidai à passer le lac, ses eaux

étoient sombres et dormantes, j'apper-
-cevois bien à une certaine distance un
pont nommé [illegible] [illegible] (mais je préférai
traverser le lac à la longue route que
j'aurois été obligé de faire pour attein-
-dre le pont, en suivant les sinuosités
d'un rivage semé de rochers. j'entrai
dans l'eau, elle étoit épaisse comme
du ciment, je m'apperçus qu'il
m'étoit inutile de nager, par tout-
-mes pieds rencontrèrent le sol. Je
marchai dans le lac pendant treize
-jours. Enfin je parvins à l'autre bord.

Photo Médiathèque Jacques-Chirac, Troyes Champagne Métropole

Photo Médiathèque Jacques-Chirac, Troyes Champagne Métropole

137

La terre étoit d'une couleur foncée comme l'eau dans la quelle j'avois voyagé, une pente insensible me conduisit au pied de l'édifice que j'avois apperçu de loin, sa

forme étoit un quarré long, sur le fron_
ton. étoient gravés quelques caracté
res, semblables à ceux qu'employ
aient les Prêtres des anciens Per
_sans. l'édifice entier étoit bâti de
Basalte noir dépoli; les portes étoient
De bois. de ciprès; Elles s'ouvrirent,
pour me laisser passer; un vent_
chaud et humide s'élevant tout
à coup me poussa rapidement_
jusqu'au milieu de la salle et en
même temps referma les portes sur_
moi… Je me trouvai dans l'obscu_
rité, peu à peu, mes yeux s'accou
tumèrent au peu de lumière qui
régnoit dans cette enceinte, et je

puis distinguer les objets qui m'entou-
-raient. la voute, les parois, le plan-
-cher de la salle étoient noirs come
l'ébène, deux tableaux peints sur la
muraille fixerent mon attention.
l'un représentoit un cheval tel
que les poëtes nous peignent celui
qui causa la ruine de Troie. De
ses flancs entrouverts sortoit un
cadavre humain. L'autre peinture
offroit l'image d'un homme mort
depuis longtems, les vils-insectes
enfans de la putréfaction, s'agit-
-taient sur son visage et dévo-
-raient la substance qui les avoit
fait naître, un des bras décharnés

de la figure morte, laissoit déja ap-
-percevoir les os ; placé près du cadavre,
un homme vêtu de rouge s'efforçoit
de le relever, une étoille brilloit
sur son front, des brodequins noirs
couvroient ses jambes, trois lames
noires chargées de caracteres d'argent
etoient posées au dessus, entre et
au dessous des tableaux. Je les lus,
et m'occupai à parcourir la salle
où je devois passer neuf jours ...
Dans un coin plus obscur
se trouvoit un monceau de terre noire,
grasse et saturée de particules ani-
-males, je voulus en prendre, une
voix éclatante comme le son d'une

trompette me le défendit, il n'y à que
quatre-vingt-sept ans que cette terre est
posée dans cette salle-me dit — elle,
quand treize autres années seront
écoulées, toi et les autres enfans de
Dieu pourront en user. La voix se
tut mais les derniers sons vibrèrent
long temps dans ce temple du silence
et de la mort. Après y être resté le
temps prescrit je sortis par la porte
opposée à celle par la qu'elle j'étois
entré. Je revis la lumière, mais elle
n'étoit pas assez vive autour de la
salle noire, pour saligner mes yeux
habitués à l'obscurité. ——
Je vis avec étonnement qu'il

me falloit pour joindre les autres édifi-
-ces traverser un lac plus large que le
premier, je marchai dans l'eau pen-
-dant dix huit jours. Je me souvins
que dans la première traversée les
eaux du lac devenoient plus noires
et plus épaisses à mesure que j'avan-
-çois, au contraire dans celle ici
plus j'approchais de la rive, et plus
les eaux s'éclaircissoient. Ma robe
qui dans le palais étoit devenue
noire comme les murailles me parut
alors d'une teinte grisâtre, elle reprit
peu à peu ses couleurs, cependant
elle n'étoit pas entièrement bleue,
mais approchant d'un beau verd.

Après dix-huit jours je montai sur le rivage par un perron de
marbre blanc ; la salle est nommée.
צחן le premier lac ראש צחן
le second אחריח צחן

Photo Médiathèque Jacques-Chirac, Troyes Champagne Métropole

145

À quelque distance du
rivage un palais somptueux élevoit
dans les airs ses colonnes d'albâtre,
ses différentes parties étoient jointes
par des portiques couleur de feu, tous

l'édifice étoit d'une architecture légère,
et aérienne. Je m'approchai des portes,
sur le fronton étoit représenté un
papillon. Les portes étoient ouvertes...
J'entrai, le palais entier ne formoit
qu'une seule salle... trois rangs de
colonnes l'entouroient, chaque rang
étoit composé de vingt sept colon-
_ nes d'albâtre. Au centre de l'édifice
étoit une figure d'homme, elle sortoit
d'un tombeau sa main appuyée
sur une lance frappoit la pierre
qui la renfermoit autrefois, une dra-
_perie verte, ceignoit ses reins l'or
brilloit au bas de son vêtement
sur sa poitrine étoit une table

quarrée, sur laqu'elle je distinguai
quelques lettres. Au dessus de la figure
étoit suspendue une couronne d'or,
elle sembloit s'élever dans les airs
pour la saisir. Au dessus de la
couronne étoit une table de pierre
jaune, sur la qu'elle étoient gravés
quelques emblêmes, je les expliquai
par le secours de l'inscription que j'ap-
-perçus sur le tombeau, et par celle
que j'avois vûe sur la poitrine de
l'homme. Je restai dans cette salle
appellée S. I ... le temps nécessaire
pour en contempler tous les détours.
et j'en sortis bientôt dans l'intention

de me rendre à travers une vaste
plaine à une tour que j'apperçus
à une assez grande distance.

A peine j'avois quitté les
marches du palais, que j'apperçus
voltiger devant moi un oiseau sem-
-blable à אספירבא mais celui ci avoit
deux ailes de papillon outre les siennes,

151

une voix sortant d'un nuage m'ordoña
de le saisir et de l'attacher. Je m'élan-
-çai après lui, il ne voloit pas mais il
se servoit de ses ailes pour courir avec
la plus grande rapidité; je le poursuivis,
il fuyoit devant moi et me fit plusieurs
fois parcourir la plaine dans toute son
étendue, Je le suivis sans m'arreter —
enfin après neuf jours de course je
le contraignis d'entrer dans la tour
que j'avois vû de loin en sortant des
— אות les murailles de ces
édifice étoit de fer. trente-six pilliers
de même métal les soutenoit, l'inté-
-rieur étoit de même matiere, incrus_
té d'acier brillant. Les fondemens

De la tour étoient construits de telle
manière que sa hauteur étoit doublée
sous terre. à peine l'oiseau fus-il en-
-tré dans cette enceinte qu'un froid
glacial sembla s'emparer de lui il fit
de vains efforts pour mouvoir ses ailes
engourdies. Il s'agitloit encore, essay-
-ait de fuir, mais si foiblement que
je l'atteignis avec la plus grande facilité.

Je le saisis, et lui passant
un clou d'acier à travers les ailes je
l'attachai sur le plancher de la tour
à l'aide d'un marteau appellé زبلي
à peine avois-je fini que l'oiseau re-
-prit de nouvelles forces, il ne s'agitla
plus, mais ses yeux devinrent

‡ פרחננחוש

brillants comme des topazes j'étois
occupé à l'examiner quand un grou-
-pe placé au centre de la salle
attira mon attention, il représentoit
un bel homme dans la fleur de
l'âge il tenoit à la main une verge
qu'entouraient deux serpens entre-
-lacés, et s'efforçait de s'échapper
des mains d'un autre homme grand
et vigoureux, armé d'une ceinture
et d'un casque de fer sur lequel
flottoit une aigrette rouge; une épée
étoit près de lui elle étoit appuyée
sur un bouclier chargé d'hiéroglyphes;
l'homme armé tenoit dans ses mains
une forte chaine il en lioit les pieds

Photo Médiathèque Jacques-Chirac, Troyes Champagne Métropole

154

en le corps de l'adolescent qui cherchait vainement à fuir son terrible ad_versaire; deux tables rouges renfer_maient des caractères.

Je quittai, la tour en ouvrant une porte qui se trouvait entre deux pillers je me trouvai dans une vaste salle.

Photo Médiathèque Jacques-Chirac, Troyes Champagne Métropole

La salle dans la qu'elle je
venois d'entrer étoit exactement ron-
de, elle ressembloit à l'intérieur d'une
boule, composée d'une matiere dure
et diaphane comme le cristal —
elle recevoit du jour par toutes ses.

parties. La partie inférieure, étoit_
posée sur un vaste bassin rempli
de sable rouge, une chaleur douce_
et égale régnoit dans cette ence_
_inte circulaire. Les sages nomment
cette salle זהריאון le bassin de sable
qui la soutient porte le nom de
אשא-חריות je considerois avec étoñement
ce globe de cristal quand un phéno_
mène nouveau excita mon admira
_tion: du plancher de la salle s'éleva
une vapeur douce, moite et safra_
née elle m'environna, me souleva
doucement et dans l'espace de
trente six jours me porta jusqu'a
la partie supérieure du globe, après

ce temps la vapeur s'affaiblit, je
descendis peu à peu enfin je me
retrouvai sur le plancher. ma robe
changea de couleur, elle étoit verte
lorsque j'entrai dans la salle, elle
devint alors d'une couleur rouge
éclatante. Par un effet contraire
le sable sur lequel reposait le
globe, quitta sa couleur rouge et
devint noir par dégrés je demeu-
-rai encore trois jours dans la
salle après la fin de mon ascension.
Après ce temps j'en sortis
pour entrer dans une vaste place
environnée de colonnades et de por-
-tiques dorés au milieu de la place étoit

un pied d'estal de bronze, il supportoit
un grouppe qui présentoit l'image
d'un homme grand et fort, sa tête
majestueuse étoit couverté d'un cas-
-que couronné; à travers les mailles
de son armure d'or, sortoit un
vêtement bleu; il tenoit d'une
main un bâton blanc, chargé de
caracteres, et tendoit l'autre à une
belle femme; aucun vêtement ne
couvroit sa compagne, un soleil
brilloit sur son sein, sa main
droite supportoit trois globes joints
par des anneaux d'or; une couroñe
de fleurs rouges ceignoit ses beaux
cheveux, elle s'élançoit dans les

airs elle sembloit y élever avec elle le
guerrier qui l'accompagnoit ; tous
les deux étoient portés sur des nuages
autour du groupe, sur les chapiteaux
de quatre colonnes de marbre blanc,
étoient posées quatre statues de bron_
_ze ; elles avoient des ailes et parois-
_saient, sonner de la trompette.

Je traversai la place, et mon_
_tant un perron de marbre qui se
trouvoit devant moi, je vis avec
étonnement que je rentrois dans la
salle des thrônes, (la première où je
m'étois trouvé en arrivant au pa_
lais de la sagesse) l'autel triangu
_laire étoit toujours au centre de celle

salle mais l'oiseau, l'autel et le flambeau
étoient reunis et ne formoient plus
qu'un corps. Près deux étois, posé
un soleil d'or, l'épée que j'avois ap-
-porté de la salle de feu, reposoit a
quel que pas delà sur le coussin d'un
des thrônes; je pris l'épée et frapant
le soleil je le réduisis en poussiere,
je le touchai ensuite et chaque mo-
-lécule devint un soleil d'or sembla-
-ble à celui que j'avois brisé. l'oeuvre
est parfait s'écria à l'instant une
voix forte et mélodieuse, à ce cri
les enfans dela lumière s'empresse-
-rent de venir me joindre, les portes
de l'immortalité me furent ouvertes,

*le nuage qui couvre les yeux des mor_
tels, se dissipa, Je Vis en les esprits
qui président aux élémens, me re_
_connurent pour leur maître.*

FIN.

Mars EL

Lecomte

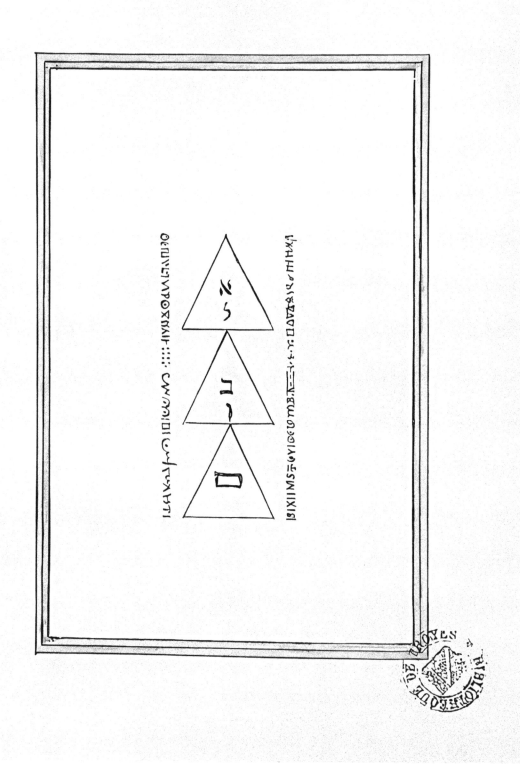

Photo Médiathèque Jacques-Chirac, Troyes Champagne Métropole

164

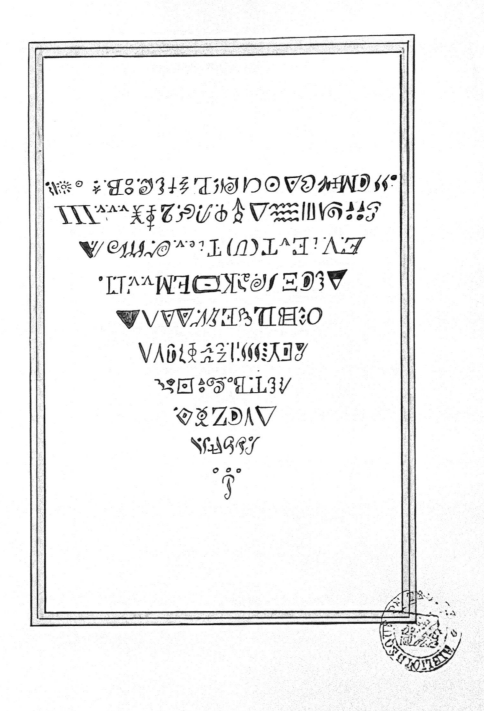

Photo Médiathèque Jacques-Chirac, Troyes Champagne Métropole

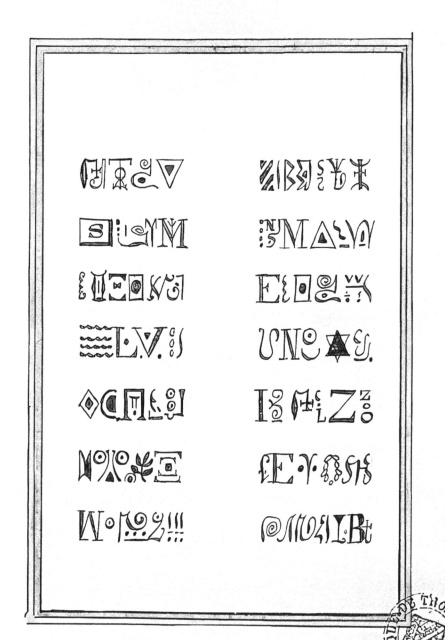

Photo Médiathèque Jacques-Chirac, Troyes Champagne Métropole

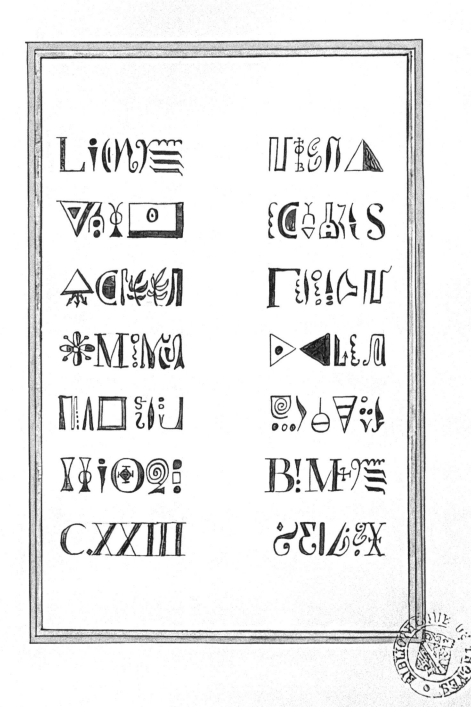

167

Photo Médiathèque Jacques-Chirac, Troyes Champagne Métropole

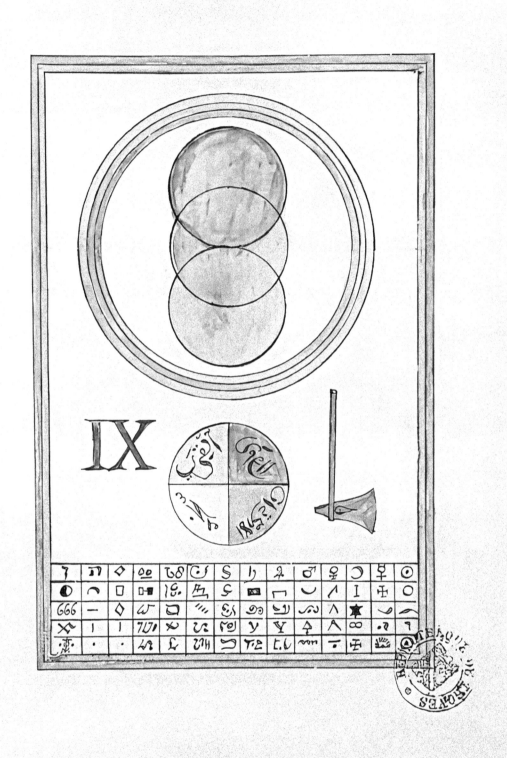

A TRANSLATION

of

THE MOST HOLY TRINOSOPHIA

otherwise known as

THE MOST HOLY THREEFOLD

WISDOM

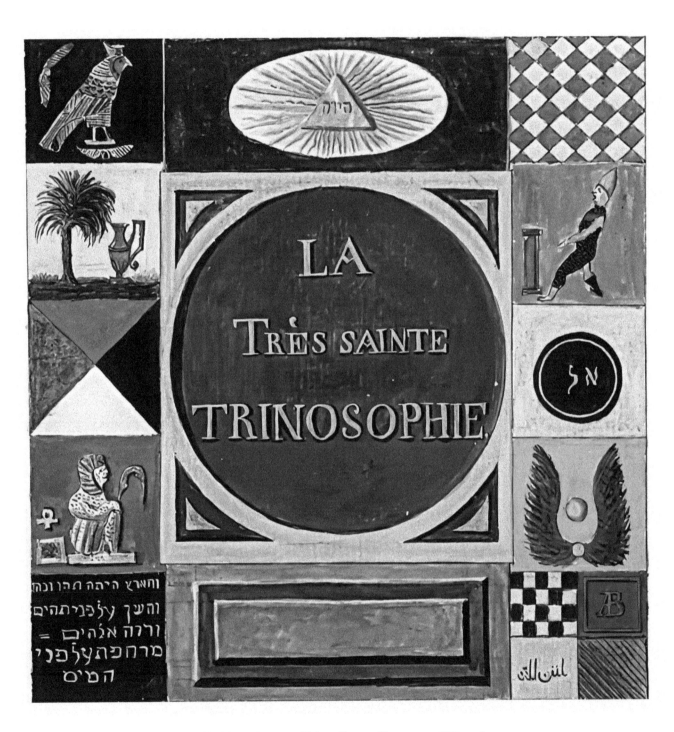

Photo Médiathèque Jacques-Chirac, Troyes Champagne Métropole

C'est dans l'azile des criminels dans les cachots de L'Inquisition, que votre ami trace ces lignes qui doivent servir à votre instruction. En songeant aux aux avantages inapréciables que doit vous, vous procurer ces écrits de l'amitié, je

It is in this Exile of Criminals, in the dungeon of the Inquisition, that your friend writes these lines for your instruction. I contemplate the inappreciable benefit that writing in friendship brings me, in softening the horrors I feel at such a long, undeserved captivity. I am happy to think that surrounded by guards and chained with irons, a slave can still raise his friend above the powerful monarchs who rule this place of exile.

My dear Philocales[43], you are going to enter the sanctuary of the sublime sciences, and my hand will lift for you the impenetrable veil the Tabernacle in the Sanctuary concealed from the eyes of the vulgar, where the Eternal deposited the secrets of nature. These are secrets reserved for a few privileged beings, the chosen ones that His Almighty power created, so that they could see and be with him in the immensity of His Glory, and direct onto the human species the rays which shine around his Golden Throne.

May the example of your friend be a salutary lesson for you. I shall therefore bless the long years of trial the wicked have put me through.

Two equally dangerous and constant pitfalls will present themselves on your path. The first would outrage the sacred rights of every individual, for it is the abuse of the power that God entrusts to you. The second would cause you loss,

---

[43] The translator misread the name in Manly P. Hall's translation, reading an 'l' as a 't'. As a result, he was called 'Philochate' or 'Philochatus'. However, the name is clearly 'Philocale', or 'Philocales' in English, meaning a lover of good.

for it is indiscretion. Both were born from the same mother, and both owe their existence to Pride. Human weakness suckled them, for they are blind and their mother, Pride, leads them. By her help these two monsters pour their impure breath even into the hearts of the Elect of the Very High. There is misfortune for him who abuses the gifts of Heaven to serve his passions, and the Almighty Hand which subjected him to the elements will break him like a weak reed in an eternity of torment, to atone for his crime. The evil spirits will smile disdainfully at the tears of the man whose threatening voice so often made them tremble within their fiery abyss.

It is not for you, Philocales, that I am painting this frightening picture. The friend of humanity will never become its persecutor, but indiscretion and the pressing need to inspire astonishment and admiration are the precipice that I dread for you. God leaves men to take care of punishing the imprudent minister who allows the eye of the profane to penetrate the mysterious Sanctuary. Oh, Philocales! May my misfortunes be forever in your mind. For I too have known happiness, filled with the blessings of Heaven surrounded by a power such that human understanding cannot conceive, commanding the spirits who rule this world, happy with the blessings that I created. I experienced the warmth of an adoring family, and the happiness which the Eternal grants to his cherished children. One moment destroyed everything. I spoke, and everything vanished like a cloud. Oh, my son, do not follow in my footsteps. Do not let any vain desire that shines in the eye of the world cause your downfall. Think of me in this dungeon, with my body broken by torture, as I write to you in friendship.

Philocales, think of the hand which traces these characters, and bears the oppressive imprint of my chains. God has punished me, but what have I done to the cruel men who persecute me? What right do they have to question the minister of the Lord? They ask me: "what are the proofs of your mission?" My witnesses are my wonders, my defender is my virtue, a life of integrity and a pure heart. What am I saying is that I still have the right to complain – and I have spoken. The Most High delivered me in weakness to the fury of fanatics, and the arm which once could overthrow an army can today hardly even lift the chains which weigh it down.

I am lost, yet I must give thanks to eternal Justice. The vengeful God has forgiven his repentant child. An aerial spirit has crossed the walls that separate me from the world. Shining with light he stood before me and fixed the end of my captivity. In two years, my misfortunes will end. My executioners will enter my dungeon and will find it empty. I will soon be purified by the four elements and made as pure as the spirits of fire. I will regain the glorious rank to which Divine goodness elevates me. Yet how far this term still is, how long two years seem to him who spends them in suffering, in humiliation. Not content to make me suffer the most horrible torture, my persecutors have employed a torment more complete and more odious still – they have called infamy on my head, they have made my name an object of shame. The children of men recoil in fear whenever they approach the walls of my prison, and they fear that a deadly vapour will escape through the narrow openings which let pass even a ray of light into my dungeon. Oh, Philocales! This is the cruellest blow they could inflict on me.

I do not yet know if I will be able to send you this book. I judge the difficulties I will experience and overcome in finishing it and getting it out of this place of turmoil, deprived of any help. I composed the materials which were necessary for me. By fire of my lamp, some coins and a few chemicals that escaped the scrutiny of my tormentors, I have produced the colours that adorn this fruit of a prisoner's leisure.

Take heed of your hapless friend's instructions. They are so clear that I fear this writing may fall into other hands than yours. Just remember that everything must serve you. A poorly explained line and a forgotten character will prevent you from lifting the veil that the hand of the Creator has placed upon the Sphinx.

Farewell, Philocales. Do not pity me, the Lord's mercy equals his righteousness. At the first mysterious assembly you will see your friend again. Praise God, I will soon give the kiss of peace to my brother.

assemblée mystérieuse, vous reverez
votre ami. Je vous salue en Dieu,
bientôt je donnerai le baiser de
paix à mon frère.

Photo Médiathèque Jacques-Chirac, Troyes Champagne Métropole

Photo Médiathèque Jacques-Chirac, Troyes Champagne Métropole

Il étoit nuit la lune cachée—
par des nuages sombres ne jettoit qu'une—
lueur incertaine. sur les blocs de lave—
qui environnent la Solfatare, la tête—
couverte du voile de Lin, tenant dans—
mes mains le rameau d'or je m'avançais

It was night and the moon was hidden by dark clouds, which cast only an uncertain glow on the blocks of lava that surround the Solfatara.[44] My head was covered in a linen veil, and I was holding a golden branch. I walked forward without fear towards the place where I had been ordered to spend the night. I was walking on hot sand, which gave way under my feet. Lightning silhouetted the gathering clouds, giving them a bloody tint like the flames of a volcano. Finally, I arrived, and found an iron altar. Here I placed the mysterious branch. I pronounced the dreadful words, and instantly the earth trembled under my feet. Thunder broke out of roaring Vesuvius in response to the quakes, and its fires joined the lightning. Choirs of genii rose into the air to make the echoes repeat the praises of the Creator.

The consecrated branch that I had placed on the Triangular Altar suddenly ignited into a thick smoke which surrounded me, so that I was no longer able to see. Plunged into darkness, I seemed to descend into an abyss. I do not know how long I remained in this situation, but upon opening my eyes I looked in vain for the objects which had previously surrounded me. The altar, Vesuvius, and the countryside of Naples had vanished from my sight, and I was in a vast underground passage, alone, far from the whole world. Near me was a long, white garment, its loose fabric seemed to be composed of linen. Also, near me on a block of granite was a copper lamp, upon a black table covered with Greek letters, which indicated to me the route I should follow. After taking the lamp

---

[44] The *Solfatara* is a shallow volcanic crater at Pozzuoli near Naples. It is part of the Phlegraean Fields volcanic area.

and putting on the garment, I entered a narrow passage whose walls were made of black marble. It was three miles long, and my footsteps echoed in a frightening manner in these silent vaults. Finally, I found a door which led to some steps which I descended. After walking for a long time, I thought I saw a moving light ahead of me, so I hid my lamp and watched the light until it vanished like a shadow.

Without reproaching the past and without fear of the future, I continued my journey. It became more and more painful, confined as I was in galleries composed of large black stones. I refrained from guessing the length of my underground journey, until finally and after an immense walk I arrived at a square chamber. A door opened in the middle of each of its four walls, which were of different colours, and each was placed at one of the four cardinal points. I entered by the door in the north side, which was black. The door to the south facing me was red, the east door was blue, and the one opposite to the west was a dazzling white.

In the centre of the room was a square block with a crystal star shining in its centre. There was a painting of a woman naked from the waist[45] on the north side. She wore a black skirt to her knees, and two bands of silver adorned her clothing. In her hand was a wand[46]. She rested it on the forehead of a man facing

---

[45] Isis.
[46] The symbol of air.

her. A table with a single leg stood between them, with a cup[47] and a spearhead[48]. A flame rose from the ground which seemed to be pointing at the man. An inscription explained the painting,[49] and another told me the means I should use to get out of the chamber.[50]

Having considered the painting and the star I wanted to pass through the red door, but as I was about to enter it turned on its hinges with a terrible noise and closed in front of me. I then tried to pass through the blue door as it was still open, but a sudden noise made me turn and I saw the star move, detach itself, revolve and quickly shoot through the opening of the white door. I immediately followed it.

---

[47] The symbol of water.
[48] The symbol of fire.
[49] Manly P. Hall states that these characters signify the Light of God and are a formula for the composition of gold - the philosopher's stone of alchemy.
[50] The top panel describes the awakening of the soul in Aries. The bottom panel in Hebrew is translated by Manly P. Hall as "on account of distress they shall cling to the Bestower."

décoroit la couleur du ciel, elle ne se
ferma point mais un bruit soudain
me fit détourner la tête, je vis —
l'étoile s'agitter, elle se détache roule
et se plonge rapidement dans —
l'ouverture dela porte blanche, je
la suivis aussitôt.

Photo Médiathèque Jacques-Chirac, Troyes Champagne Métropole

Photo Médiathèque Jacques-Chirac, Troyes Champagne Métropole

Un vent impétueux s'é
leva, jeus peine à conserver ma
lampe allumée enfin un perron
de marbre blanc s'offrit à ma
que j'y montai par neuf marches

A fierce wind started, and I struggled to keep my lamp alight. Eventually I saw a white marble staircase with nine steps. I climbed the steps and on the last one I saw an immense expanse of water. To my right I heard furious torrents of water, and on my left cold rain and balls of hail fell near me. I was contemplating this majestic scene when the star which had guided me through the door - and which was swinging slowly overhead - plunged into the depths. Thinking that I was following orders from above, I rushed into the midst of the waves, where an invisible hand seized my lamp and placed it on the top of my head. I swam in the foaming wave and strove to reach the opposite shore. Finally, in the horizon I saw a faint light, and I hastened to reach it. I was in the middle of the water and sweat covered my face as I exhausted myself in a vain effort to reach the shore that I could hardly see, and which seemed to flee before me as I advanced. My strength abandoned me. I was not afraid of dying, but of dying without being enlightened. I lost courage and looked up with tears in my eyes, exclaiming: "Pass judgment and redeem me, by your power let me live".[51]

I could barely move my tired limbs and sank deeper and deeper. Then I saw a boat near me, rowed by a man covered in rich clothes. I noticed that the bow was turned towards the shore I had left. He approached me, a golden crown shone on his forehead: "Come with me, the greatest prince in the world, and I will show you the way to follow."[52] I answered him at once: "it is better to trust

---

[51] The text: "*Judica judicum meum et redime me, propter eloquim tuum vivifica me.*"
[52] The text: "*vade mecum, mecum principium in terris, instruamte in via hac qua gradueris.*"

the Lord than to trust in any prince."[53] Immediately the boat sank, with the prince in it. Fresh energy flowed through my veins, and I managed to achieve my goal. I found myself on the opposite shore, which had green sand. A silver wall inlaid with two slabs of red marble was in front of me. I approached and saw that one was inscribed with sacred characters[54], and the other was engraved with a line of Greek letters. Between the two slabs was an iron circle with two lions one red[55], and the other black[56], resting on clouds. Above them was a golden crown.[57] I could see near the circle a bow and two arrows[58]. I read some characters written on the sides of one of the lions[59]. I had scarcely considered these emblems when the wall that contained them disappeared.

---

[53] The text: *"bonum est sperare in Domino quam considere in principibus."*
[54] A Dionysian prayer, translated by Manly P. Hall as: "Each must sprinkle himself with his own wine from the mountain of Chios. He must drink to God before the wood. He must give himself in exchange for that which he yearns."
[55] Lust.
[56] Tyranny.
[57] Kether.
[58] To slay ambition.
[59] Inverted, symbolising the perversion of power.

voyois encore près du cercle un arc
et deux flèches je lus quelques
caracteres écrits sur les flancs d'un
des lions. à peine avait je observé ces
differens emblêmes, qu'ils disparu-
rent avec la muraille qui les
contenait.

Photo Médiathèque Jacques-Chirac, Troyes Champagne Métropole

A sa place un lac de feu
se présenta devant moi, le soufre
et le bitume roulaient leurs flots
enflammés je frémis, une voix
éclatante m'ordonna de traverser.

In place of the wall a lake of fire appeared before me. Sulphur and asphalt rolled in flaming waves. I shuddered as a resounding voice ordered me to cross through the flames. I obeyed, and the flames appeared to have lost their heat. I walked for a long time through the fire before I arrived at a circular hall. Here I contemplated the beautiful spectacle, which the goodness of Heaven was given me to enjoy.

Forty columns of fire decorated the hall I was in. One side of the columns glowed with a bright white fire, the other appeared shadowy, covered with a blackish flame. In the centre of this place stood an altar in the shape of a snake. A greenish gold embellished its variegated scales, which reflected the flames surrounding it[60]. Its eyes looked like rubies, and a silver inscription was placed near it[61]. A lavish sword was stuck in the ground near the serpent, and a cup rested on its head[62]. I heard the choir of celestial spirits, and a voice said to me: "the end of your work is approaching, take the sword, strike the serpent."

I drew the sword from its scabbard and approached the altar. Taking the cup with one hand, I struck a terrible blow on the neck of the serpent with the other. The sword rebounded, and the blow sounded as if I had struck a brass bell. Hardly had I obeyed the voice when the altar disappeared, and the columns vanished. The sound which I had heard when striking the altar repeated as if a

---

[60] The serpent of desire.
[61] Trans. by Manly P. Hall as: "Reverence this vessel of Everlastingness; offer freely of yourself a portion unto God and go to the corner in atonement."
[62] The cup of immortality.

thousand blows were struck at the same time. A hand seized me by the hair and lifted me towards the ceiling, which opened to let me through. Shadowy phantoms appeared to me, hydras, lamias[63] and other serpents surrounded me. The sight of the sword in my hand swept away this filthy crowd, just as the first rays of day dispel nightmares and frail dream-children of the night. After climbing upwards through the different layers that make up the walls of the earth, I saw the light of day again.

---

[63] Translator: in ancient Greek mythology a lamia was a child-eating monster or sometimes a haunting demon.

les songes frêles enfans dela nuits.
Après être monté par une ligne
perpendiculaire à travers les
couches qui composent les parrois
du globe. Je revis la lumiere du
Jour.

אשא

חלים

Photo Médiathèque Jacques-Chirac, Troyes Champagne Métropole

À peine étais-je parvenu à la surface de la terre, que mon con- ducteur invisible m'entraîna plus rapidement encore, la vélocité avec la qu'elle nous parcourions les —

Once I had reached the surface of the earth, my invisible guide carried me much faster. The speed with which we traversed space cannot be compared to anything else. In an instant I lost sight of the plains over which I was flying. I observed with astonishment that I emerged from the middle of the earth and was far from the countryside around Naples. A desert with a few triangular structures were the only objects I could discern. Soon, despite the hardships I had undergone, a new terror assailed me, as the earth seemed to me to be no more than a vague cloud. I was raised to an immense height by my invisible guide who then abandoned me, and I fell for quite a long time, rolling in space. The earth appeared closer to my troubled eyes, and I was calculating how many minutes would pass before I smashed onto its rocks. As I was thinking this, my guide swiftly rushed after me and took me away once again, upwards to an immeasurable distance. I saw planets around me, and earths gravitate at my feet. Suddenly the spirit carrying me touched my eyes and I blacked out.

I do not know how long I spent in this state but, when I woke up, I found myself lying on a plush pillow breathing in fresh air scented with flowers and herbs. A garment, strewn with gold stars, had replaced my white linen gown. Close to me was a golden altar, from which a pure flame burned without any fuel to sustain it. Black characters were engraved on its base[64]. Nearby was a lighted torch that

---

[64] Trans. By Manly P. Hall as: "when shall be the gate or entrance."

shone like the sun. Above it was a bird[65] whose feet and wings were black[66], its body silver[67], its head red[68], and its neck golden[69]. It moved constantly but without using its wings. It could only fly when it was amid the flames. In its beak was a green branch whose name is *"Hakim"*[70].

The name of the altar is *"Hallaj"*[71].

The altar, the bird and the torch are the symbols of everything, nothing can be done without them - they themselves are all that is good and great.

The torch is *"Majûsî-Mazdéen"*[72]

---

[65] Ibis, the symbol of Thoth.
[66] Earth.
[67] Water.
[68] Fire.
[69] Air.
[70] Trans. By Manly P. Hall as: "to be given the life." It signifies the Crown, or Kether. In old Turkish, the word and the name Hâkim also mean "the Judge."
[71] Trans. "the weaver." Manly P. Hall states that the import of the word is: "here shall be the gate or entrance".
[72] "Light".

Four inscriptions surrounded these different emblems.

se nomme. Quatre inscriptions en
_ raient ces différents emblèmes.

Photo Médiathèque Jacques-Chirac, Troyes Champagne Métropole

J e me détournai et j'apperçus un palais immense, sa baze reposoit sur des nuages, des marbres
composaient sa masse; sa forme
étoit triangulaire quatre étages de

I turned away and saw an immense palace. Its base rested on clouds, and it was made of marble. Its shape was triangular with four storeys of columns rising one above the other. A golden ball topped the structure. The first row of columns was white; the second black; the third green; and the last was a brilliant red. After admiring this work of immortal artists, I wanted to return to the place where the altar, the bird and the torch were. I still wanted to observe them, but they were gone.

I looked for them when the doors of the palace opened. A venerable old man came out. His robe was similar to mine, except that a golden sun shone on his chest. In his right hand he held a green branch, and in the other a censer. A wooden chain was attached to his collar and a pointed tiara like that of Zoroaster covered his white hair. He approached me with the smile of kindness and said:

> *"Adore God" in Persian. "It is He who supported you in the trials,"* he
> *continued, "His spirit was with you. My son, you let the opportunity slip*
> *away. You could at that moment have grasped the bird,*[73]

---

[73] Aspirka.

"the torch"[74],

"and the altar"[75].

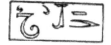

"You would have become the altar, bird and torch. Now, to reach the most secret place and sublime palace of science, you must go through all the tests. Come, I must first introduce you to my brothers."

He took my hand and led me into a large hall. Ordinary eyes cannot conceive the form and the richness of the ornaments which embellished it. Three hundred and sixty columns surrounded it on all sides. On the ceiling was a red, white, blue, and black cross suspended from a gold ring. In the centre of the hall was a Triangular Altar composed of the four elements. On its three points were placed the bird, the altar and the torch.

---

[74] Majûsi, "Light".
[75] Hâkim, "Immortality".

"They have changed their names", my guide told me. "Here we call the bird "Aspirka"[76]

אספּיךכא

"the altar we call "Kahuna"[77],

"and the torch we call "Gephrîth"[78]

"the hall we call "Hajalah"[79]

"the Triangular Altar we call "Athanor""[80]

---

[76] "Diligence".
[77] Cohen or "Priesthood".
[78] Brimstone or Sulphur.
[79] "The Bridal Suite".
[80] An *athanor* is a furnace used to provide constant heat for alchemical reduction. The word descends from the Arabic term "*al-tannoor*", a bread-oven.

Around the altar were placed eighty-one thrones; each with nine steps of unequal height covered in red carpet. As I examined the thrones, the sound of a trumpet was heard and the doors of the hall *Hajalah*

opened, to let seventy-nine men pass, all dressed in the same way as my guide. They slowly approached and sat down on the thrones, my guide standing alongside me. An old man, distinguished from his brothers by a purple cloak, the edges of which were loaded with embroidered characters, stood up. My guide speaking in the sacred language said: "this is one of our children, whom God wants to make as great as his fathers. May the will of the Lord be accomplished." The old man then said to me: "My son, the time of your physical trials is over."

My guide continued: "Nonetheless, you still have to make great journeys, but from now on you will be called *"El-Taam"*[81]

---

[81] "Wise-Man" or shaman. The root word is the Hebrew *ta'am*, is to perceive, experience, and be nourished.

"Before you walk through this building, eight of my brothers and I are going to each give you a present." He came to me and gave me the kiss of peace and a cube of grey earth, called *"Humam"*[82]

The second, three cylinders of black stone called *"Qenka"*[83]

קֶבֶךְ

The third was a rounded piece of crystal[84]

The fourth was a plume of blue feathers called *"Ashqûshaq"*

---

[82] Human. Ash or lava from a volcano.
[83] Nest, or grave. The astrological symbol is the Moon.
[84] The meaning is not known. The astrological symbol is Mercury.

The fifth added a silver vessel called "*Geshem*"[85]

בשם

The sixth was a bunch of grapes known among the wise as "*Marah-Resha*"[86]

בוזה רשא

The seventh presented me with a figure of a bird called "*Ever*" similar in shape to [the bird on the altar], but it did not have the same brilliant colours, but was silver. "It wears the same name," he said to me, "it is up to you to give it the same virtues."

הזוי

The eighth gave me a small altar also resembling the altar, called "*Nephrith*"

---

[85] The astrological symbol is the Sun. Lit. "gold body."
[86] *Marah-resha*: the first of the two words means "bitterness"; the second a Chaldaic form of *rasch*, "head:". The astrological symbol is Jupiter or Mars.

נְפִירִית

Finally, my conductor put in my hand a torch made up of shining particles of light called "Marah"

פְרוּה

but it was extinguished. "It is up to you," he added, "just like those who have preceded you, to give this the same virtues. Reflect on these gifts. The wise strive for perfection, but no one is perfect. It is from your existing form that the divine work must emerge. Know also that all these gifts are useless if you do not use them according to the order in which they were given to you. The second without the first would be only a raw material without heat, utility, or the help of the one which comes after it. Keep these presents carefully and begin your journey after drinking from the cup of life." He then presented me a crystal cup, with a brilliant and saffron liquor of exquisite fragrance which tasted delicious. I wanted to return the cup after dipping my lips into the liquor, but the old man said: "finish this beverage. it will be the only food you will take during your journey." I obeyed and I felt a divine fire run through all the fibres of my body. I was stronger, more courageous, and even my intellectual faculties seemed to have doubled. I hastened to give the salute of the wise to the august assembly as I left, and on

the orders of my guide entered a long gallery on my right.

avoir trempé mes levres dans la liqueur
achève me dit le vieillard, ce breuvage
sera la seule nourriture que tu prendras
pendant le temps de tes voyages. J'obéis
et je sentis un feu divin parcourir
tous les fibres de mon corps, j'étois plus
forts, plus courageux, mes facultés même
intellectuelles, semblaient être doublées.

Je me hâtai de donner le salut des
sages à l'auguste assemblée que j'allais
quitter, et par les ordres de mon conduc-
-teur, je m'enfonçai dans une longue
galerie qui se trouvoit à ma droite.

Photo Médiathèque Jacques-Chirac, Troyes Champagne Métropole

Photo Médiathèque Jacques-Chirac, Troyes Champagne Métropole

A l'entrée de la galerie dans
la qu'elle je me trouvois étoit posée une
cuve d'acier, a mon approche elle se
remplit d'une eau pure côme le cris_
_tal, qui vint s'épurer sur un sable. _

A steel bath was placed at the entrance to the long gallery in which I found myself. Approaching, I found it filled with water as pure as crystal purified by fine white sand. The bath was oval and supported by three brass feet. A black panel on the side facing the door I entered contained a several characters. Near the bath was a linen veil.

Above it, two green marble columns supported a round marble panel. There were two inscriptions, and the image of a sacred seal formed of a cross of four colours, attached to a gold crossbar supporting two circles, which surrounded two other concentric circles, the larger black, the other red[87].

On one of the columns was attached a silver axe with a blue shaft called "*Qualqanthûm*"[88]

קלקנתום

After reading the inscriptions[89], I approached the bath and washed myself, starting with my hands. I ended up immersing myself completely in it. I stayed

---

[87] The *Lapis Philosophorum*, composed of the regenerated elements of salt (earth), sulphur (fire), mercury (air) and ether (water).

[88]"The Destroyer." The word also designates calcanthium, or copper sulphate. The instrument of separation in alchemy.

[89] Trans. Manly P. Hall: "And the outbreathing of Everlastingness. Know that place to be the end. The leg is the beginning of the destruction." The "leg" Hall suggests is our present age, the Age of Aquarius.

there for three days. When I got out of the water, I noticed that it had lost its transparency. The sand at the bottom had turned grey, and rust-coloured particles stirred in the fluid. I wanted to dry myself with the help of the linen veil, but new drops of water constantly replaced those with which the linen soaked up. I gave up drying myself with the veil and, standing in the shade, remained there motionless for six whole days. At the end of this time, the source of the water had dried up. I found myself dry and lighter, although my strength seemed to me to be increased. After walking for some time, I returned to the bath. The water had gone; in its place was a reddish liquid, and the sand was grey and metallic. I bathed in it again, observing, however, that I only stayed there for a few moments before I got out. I saw that I had absorbed some of this liquid. This time I did not try to dry the liquid on me with the cloth, as it would have destroyed it instantly, because the liquid was strong and corrosive. I went to the other end of the gallery to lie down on a bed of warm sand and spent seven days there. At the end of this time, I returned to the bath and the water was like the first time. I got back in it and came out after washing myself carefully. This time I managed without difficulty to dry myself. Finally, after having purified myself according to the instructions I was given, I prepared to leave the gallery having been there sixteen days.

doit sorte en corrosive. Je fus à l'autre
bout de la gallerie m'étendre sur un
lit de sable chaud, j'y passai sept jours
au bout de ce temps je revins à la
cuve l'eau doit semblable a la premi-
-ere, je m'y replongeai et en ressortis
après m'être lavé avec soin. Cette fois
je parvins sans peine à m'essuyer,
enfin après m'être purifié selon
les instructions que j'avois reçu, je
me disposai à sortir de cette gale-
-rie après y être resté seize jours.

Photo Médiathèque Jacques-Chirac, Troyes Champagne Métropole

Je quittai la galerie par une
porte basse et étroite et j'entrai ___
dans un appartement circulaire
ses lambris étoient de bois de frê-
ne et de sandal. au fond de l'ap

I left the gallery via a low, narrow door and entered a circular room. Its panelling was ash tree and sandalwood. At the back of the room, on a plinth made up of vines, rested a block of shiny white salt. Above it was a painting with a crowned white lion[90] and a bunch of grapes.[91] They were placed on a tray, which the smoke of a lighted brazier raised into the air. On my right and left were two opened doors. The first opening onto an arid plain, where dry and scorching hot wind never ceased. The other door opened onto a lake, at the end of which I saw a facade of black marble.

I approached the altar and took in my hands the shiny white salt which the sages call "*Marah-Resha*".[92]

מֵוַֹח רֵישָׁא

I rubbed this all over my body, which it penetrated. After reading the hieroglyphs that accompanied the panel,[93] I prepared to leave the room. My first idea was to go out through the door that opened onto the plain, but a hot vapour blew, and I preferred the opposite path. I had the freedom to choose, with the condition, however, of not leaving the one I had taken. I decided to cross the lake. Its waters

---

[90] Aspiration.

[91] Illumination.

[92] The alchemical salt, symbolic of the immortal soul. The first of the two words means "bitterness"; the second is a Chaldaic form of *rasch*, meaning "head".

[93] Trans. Manly P. Hall. That on the right: "Kindle a light at the appointed time – the seventh hour of the dawning. Dance in the circle of prophecy." That on the left: "Honour is paid to the giver of life."

were dark and dormant. I could see in some distance a bridge named *Peut-Etre Bas*[94]

but I preferred to cross the lake rather than take the long, winding road running alongside a shore strewn with rocks leading to the bridge. I therefore entered the water, which was as thick as cement. I realized that it was useless to try and swim, as my feet touched the ground everywhere. I walked through the lake for thirteen days. Finally, I made it to the other side.

---

[94] Lit. "Low."

étoient sombres et dormantes, j'apper-
-cevois bien à une certaine distance un
pont nommé اسرافيل (mais je préférai
traverser le lac à la longue route que
j'aurois été obligé de faire pour attein-
-dre le pont, en suivant les sinuosités
d'un rivage semé de rochers. j'entrai
dans l'eau, elle étoit épaisse comme
du ciment, je m'apperçus qu'il
m'étoit inutile de nager, par tous
mes pieds rencontrèrent le sol. Je
marchai dans le lac pendant treize
jours. Enfin je parvins à l'autre bord.

Photo Médiathèque Jacques-Chirac, Troyes Champagne Métropole

Photo Médiathèque Jacques-Chirac, Troyes Champagne Métropole

La terre étoit d'une couleur
foncée comme l'eau dans la qu'elle
j'avois voyagé, une pente insensi-
-ble me conduisit au pied de l'édifi-
-ce que j'avois apperçu de loin, sa

The earth was a dark colour, like the water through which I had walked. An almost indiscernible slope led me to the foot of the building I had seen from afar. Its shape was a long square on which were engraved some characters, like those used by the priests of ancient Persia. The entire edifice was built of rough black Basalt. The doors were of cypress wood, and opened to let me in. A hot and humid wind suddenly arose and pushed me to the middle of the chamber, at the same time closed the doors behind me. I found myself in the dark, but little by little my eyes became accustomed to the dim light inside, and I could distinguish objects around me. The vault, the walls, and the floor of the hall were as black as ebony.[95] Two pictures painted onto the wall grabbed my attention. The first represented a horse like that referred to by the poets, which caused the fall of Troy. From its half-open sides came a human corpse. The second presented the image of a man who had been dead for some time. The vile insects of putrefaction agitated on his face and devoured the substance which had given birth to them. One of the gaunt arms of the dead man was stripped to the bones of its flesh. A man dressed in red stood next to the corpse and strove to raise it. A star shone on his forehead, and he had long black boots. Above, between and below were three black panels with silver characters.[96] I read them and busied myself with walking through the room, where I was to spend nine days.

---

[95] The house of putrefaction.
[96] Trans. Manly P. Hall. That at the top reads: "That which is hidden shall be brought to view". That in the middle: "the gate of the end when the Leg or the Waterman turns in the circle." He third: "Seek after the all-powerful Lord who is the Guardian of the Tree of Life."

In a dark corner was a heap of black earth, saturated with animal fat. I wanted to take some, but a voice bursting out at the sound of a trumpet forbade me. "It is only eighty-seven years that this earth has been placed in this room," it said to me, "when thirteen more years have passed, you and the other children of God will be able to use it." The voice fell silent, but the last sounds vibrated for a long time in this temple of silence and death. After staying there for the prescribed time, I left through the opposite door. I saw the light again, but it was not as bright enough around the dark hall as to strain my eyes which had become used to the darkness.

I saw with amazement that I had to cross a lake larger than the first to reach the other buildings. I walked in the water for eighteen days. I remembered that on first crossing the waters of the lake, that it had become darker and thicker as I went on; now the closer I got to the shore the clearer the waters became. My garment, which in the palace had become as black as the walls, was now of a grey tint, but gradually regained its colours. However, it was not entirely blue, but approaching a beautiful green.

After eighteen days I came to the shore by way a white marble staircase.

The dark hall is called "*Tsahn*"[97]

צַחַן

The first lake is called "*Tsahn Rosh*"[98];

צַחַן ראשׁ

and the second like is called "*Tsahn Aharith*".[99] [100]

צַחַן אחרית

---

[97] "Corruption".
[98] "Beginning of Corruption".
[99] "The End of Corruption".
[100] Manly P. Hall: the three words when read together mean: "Corruption is the beginning of decay and corruption is followed by death".

Après dix huit jours je montai sur le rivage par un perron de
marbre blanc; la salle est nomée.
צחן le premier lac צחן ראש
le second אחדיח צחן

SECTION X

Photo Médiathèque Jacques-Chirac, Troyes Champagne Métropole

228

A quel que distance du
rivage un palais somptueux élevoit
dans les airs ses colonnes d'albâtre,
ses différentes parties étoient jointes
par des portiques couleur de feu, tous

At some distance from the shore, a sumptuous palace with alabaster columns rose into the sky. Its various parts were connected by porticos of a fiery colour. The entire building was of a light and airy architecture. I approached the doors, which were decorated with a butterfly. The doors were open, and I entered. One hall formed the entire palace. Three rows of columns surrounded it, and each row was composed of twenty-seven alabaster columns. In the centre of the building was a figure of a man emerging from a tomb. In his hand he held hand a spear striking the tomb which formerly held him. Around his waist he wore a green garment edged with gold. The garment on his chest bore a square tablet on which I made out a few letters. The figure seemed to be reaching into the air to grab a golden crown suspended above it. Above the crown was a table made of yellow stone, on which were engraved some emblems. I understood them with the help of the inscription I saw on the tomb and on the man's chest.

I stayed in this hall, called *"Balsan"* 101

بهلسان ابرون

---

101 The first word seems *Balsân* "balm", the second is impossible to identify. The import of the sentence appears to be: "At the outpouring of the Almighty the persecutors shall be shut up and overcome."

for as long as I needed to contemplate its aisles, and soon left with the intention of walking across a vast plain with a tower I saw from a long distance.

De me rendre `a travers une vaste plaine `a une tour que j'apperçus `a une assez grande distance.

SECTION XI

Photo Médiathèque Jacques-Chirac, Troyes Champagne Métropole

232

À peine j'avois quitté les
marches du palais, que j'apperçus
voltiger devant moi un oiseau semblable à אספירכא mais celui ci avoit
deux ailes de papillon outre les siennes,

233

No sooner had I departed from the steps of the palace, when I saw a bird flying in front of me like Aspirka,[102]

אַסְפִּירְכָא

but this one had two butterfly wings besides its own. A voice coming out of a cloud ordered me to seize the bird and tie it up. So, I rushed after it. It was not flying but used its wings to run with the greatest speed. I pursued the bird without stopping as it fled before me across the furthest extent of the plain several times. Finally, after nine days of chasing after it, I forced it to enter the tower, called "Tsahn"[103], that I had seen as I was leaving.

צַחֻן

The walls of the tower were made of iron. There were thirty-six pillars of iron supporting it. The interior was of the same material but inlaid with shiny steel. The foundations of the tower were constructed in such a way that it was twice as deep underground as it was above. No sooner had the bird entered this enclosure when it became icy cold and was unable to move its frozen wings. It

---

[102] A mother shall bear the likeness.
[103] Corruption.

was still weakly fidgeting and trying to flee when I reached it with the greatest ease. I grabbed it and drove a steel nail called *"Marah-Nebush"* [104]

בַּרַח נָהוּשׁ

through its wings, and nailed it to the floor of the tower using a hammer called *"Shîtraj"* [105]

I had barely finished when the bird regained its strength and, while it no longer moved, its eyes began to shine like topaz. I was busy examining it when a picture in the centre of the hall caught my attention. It represented a handsome young man in the prime of life. He held in his hand a rod, surrounded by two intertwined serpents. He was trying to escape from another man, taller and more vigorous, who was armed with a belt and an iron helmet with red plumes. A sword was close by, leaning on a shield covered with hieroglyphics. The armed man held a strong chain in his hands with he was binding the feet and body of the younger man, who vainly sought to flee from his terrible adversary. Two red tablets bore some characters.

---

[104] Brassiness.
[105] To make haste.

I left the tower and, opening a door which is between two pillars, found myself in a large hall.

es la corps De l'adolescent qui cherchoit vainement 'a fuir son terrible. ad-_versaire; deux tables rouges renfer-_maient des caracteres.

Je quittai, la tour en ouvrant, une porte qui se trouvoit, entre_ Deux pillers je me trouvai dans une vaste salle.

La salle dans la qu'elle je
venois D'entrer étoit éxactement ron_
_De, elle ressembloit `a l'intérieur D'une
boule, composée D'une matiere dure
et Diaphane comme le cristal _
elle recevoit du jour par toutes ses

The hall I now entered was perfectly round and resembled the interior of a ball. It was everywhere and made of a hard and diaphanous material-like crystal and appeared to be natural. The lower part was placed on a vast basin filled with red sand. This circular structure had a gentle and even temperature. The wise men call this hall *"Zelûph"*[106]

זלרף ‎ ‏

The basin of sand which supports it bears the name *"Asha-Hôlith"*.[107]

אשא הרלית

I was gazing at the crystal globe with astonishment when a new phenomenon aroused my attention. From the floor of the room arose a soft, moist and humid Cloud. The Thing surrounded me, lifted me gently and, in the space of thirty-six days, carried me to the upper part of the globe. After this time the Cloud subsided, and I gradually descended until I eventually found myself on the ground. My garment which had been bright red when I entered the hall had changed colour and was now green. A contrary effect took place on the sand on which the globe rested, as its red colour had gradually turned black.

---

[106] The import is "a place where drops trickle."
[107] "Fire Sand." The import of the words are "the desert of blazing fire."

Following my ascension I remained in the hall three more days, after which I left to enter a vast square surrounded by colonnades and gilded porticoes. In the middle of the square was a bronze pedestal, which supported a group representing the image of a tall and strong man, whose majestic head was crowned with a helmet. Beneath the meshes of his golden armour he wore a blue garment. In one hand he held a white staff inscribed with characters, and he offered the other to a beautiful woman. No garment covered his companion, but a sun shone on her breast, and her right hand supported three globes joined by gold rings. A wreath of red flowers encircled her beautiful hair. She soared into the air, and seemed to raise the warrior accompanying her. Both were borne up by clouds surrounding the group. On the capitals of four white marble columns were placed four bronze winged statues who appeared to be playing trumpets.

I crossed the square and, ascending a marble staircase in front of me, saw with astonishment that I had re-entered the hall of thrones (where I had first found myself when I arrived at the Palace of Wisdom). The Triangular Altar was still in the centre of this room, but the bird, the altar and the flame were united and formed only one body. Next to them was a golden sun. The sword I had brought with me from the hall of fire rested a few steps away on a cushion on one of the thrones. I took the sword and struck the sun, reducing it to dust. I then touched it and each molecule became a golden sun like the one I had broken.

"The work is now made perfect!" cried out a loud and melodious voice instantly. At this cry the Children of Light hastened to come and join me, the doors of immortality were opened unto me and the cloud that covers the eyes of mortals vanished.

I saw the spirits that preside over the elements, who recognised me as their master.

THE END

le nuage qui couvre les yeux des mor_
tels, se dissipa, Je Vis en les esprits
qui présidens, aux élémens, me re_
_connurens, pour leur maître.

FIN.

Mars   EL

Lecomte

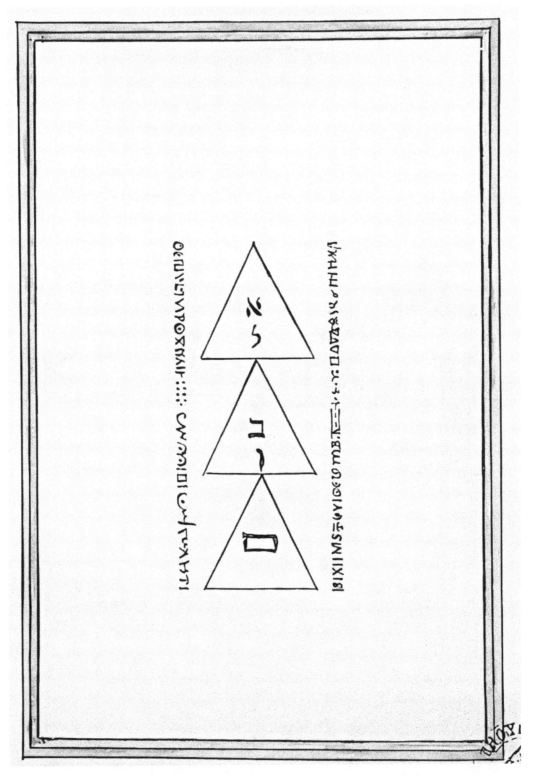

Photo Médiathèque Jacques-Chirac, Troyes Champagne Métropole

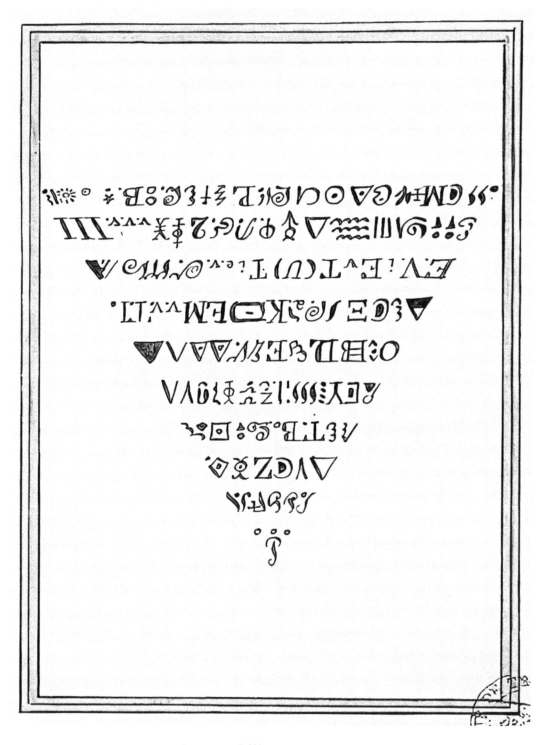

Inverted illustration[108]

Photo Médiathèque Jacques-Chirac, Troyes Champagne Métropole

244

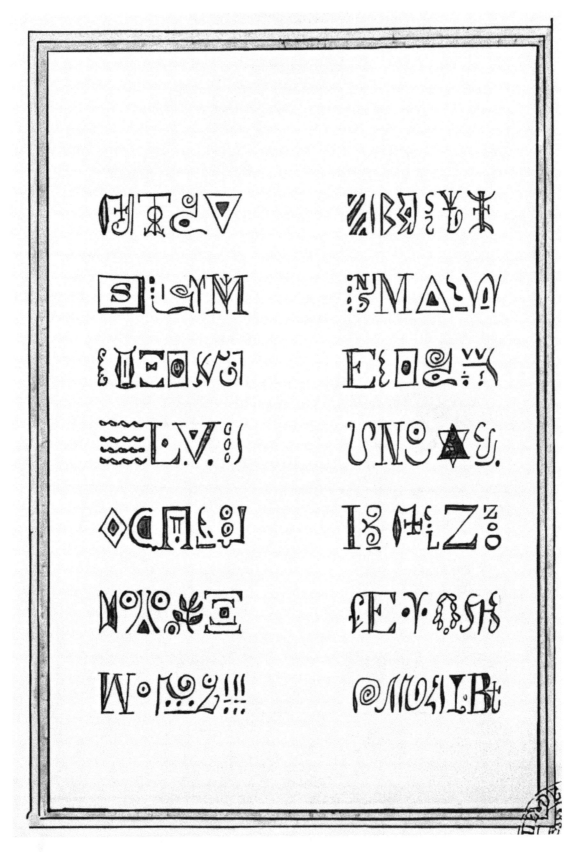

Photo Médiathèque Jacques-Chirac, Troyes Champagne Métropole

246

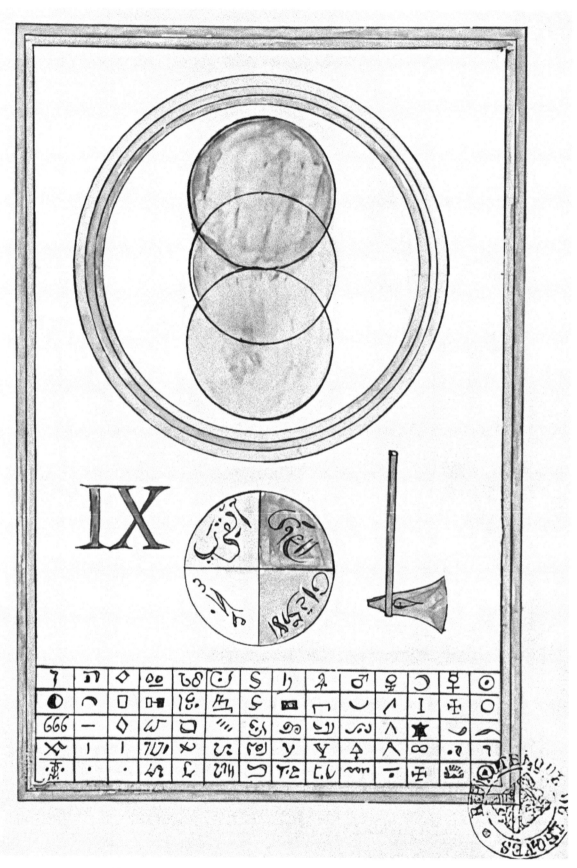

Photo Médiathèque Jacques-Chirac, Troyes Champagne Métropole

248

ACKNOWLEDGMENTS

We wish to thank the following for their kind assistance and help with this publication:

Anne-Charlotte Pivot, Conservatrice des bibliotheques, Médiathèque Jacques-Chirac

Antje Prufig, Gestion de Patrimone, Médiathèque Jacques-Chirac

Susan Noyes, Proof-Reading Services www.suenoyes.com

W.B. Steve Adams 32° K.C.C.H., image enhancement and cover design steve@pixeljitsu.com

Printed in the USA
CPSIA information can be obtained
at www.ICGtesting.com
LVHW070916051123
763093LV00012B/193